Celebrating your year

1972

a very special year for

A message from the author:

Welcome to the year 1972.

I trust you will enjoy this fascinating romp down memory lane.

And when you have reached the end of the book, please join me in the battle against AI generated copy-cat books and fake reviews.

Details are near the back of the book.

Best regards,
Bernard Bradforsand-Tyler.

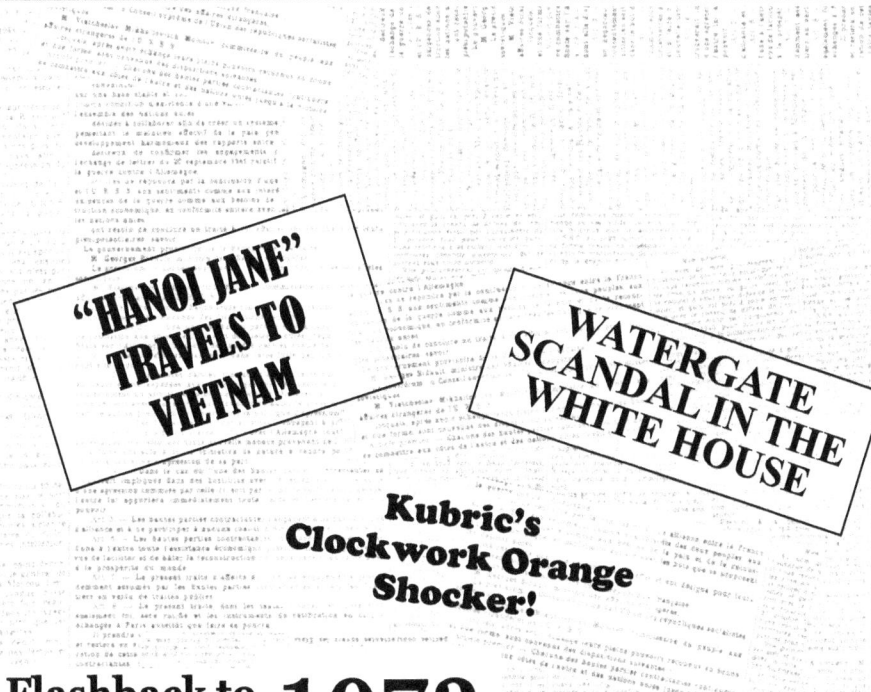

"HANOI JANE" TRAVELS TO VIETNAM

WATERGATE SCANDAL IN THE WHITE HOUSE

Kubric's Clockwork Orange Shocker!

Flashback to **1972** a very special year

PIONEER 10 BEAMS FROM JUPITER

BLOODY SUNDAY NORTHERN IRELAND

OLYMPIC MASSACRE IN MUNICH

GREASE opens on Broadway

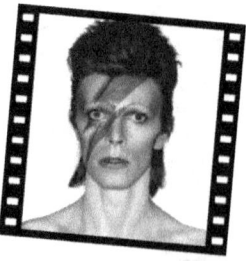

Contents

1972 Family Life in the USA 8
Life in the United Kingdom 12
Rise of the Communes 16
Our Love Affair with Automobiles 19
Clean Air for All 24
Nuclear Bomb Testing 27
Battlefield Vietnam 28
Anti-Vietnam War Sentiment 29
Watergate–Scandal in the White House . 30
Troubles in Northern Ireland–Bloody Sunday . . 32
UK Miner's and Docker's Strikes 34
Australia Sacks PM Whitlam 37
Summer Olympics 1972 38
Massacre in Munich 39
Operation Wrath of God 40
Grease Opens on Broadway 43
Tuning in to Television 44
1972 in Cinema and Film 48
Top Grossing Films of the Year 49
A Decade of Disasters 50
Musical Memories 52
1972 Billboard Top 30 Songs 54
Fashion Trends of the 1970s 58
Also in Sports 67
Technology and Medicine 69
Other News from 1972 70
Famous People Born in 1972 72
1972 in Numbers 76
Image Attributions 84

Advertisement

FOR THE COACH PASSENGER THIS IS THE MOST COMFORTABLE FLEET OF PLANES IN THE WORLD.

TWA's 707 COACH LOUNGE. NO OTHER AIRLINE HAS IT.

TWA's 747 COACH LOUNGE.

ONLY ON TWA. Completely refurnished interiors on all our 707s. New seats, carpets, fabrics, colors, etc. **ONLY ON TWA.** The Twin Seat in 707 coach. If the plane's not full, it can be three across, two across or even a couch. **ONLY ON TWA.** A choice of 2 first-run movies on every movie flight. One for general audiences, one for mature (nominal charge for movies in coach). **ONLY ON TWA.** A choice of 3 international meals in coach, 5 in first class, with wines, champagnes, liqueurs, cheeses and desserts (nominal charge for alcoholic beverages in coach).

Call your travel agent or TWA.

TWA's AMBASSADOR SERVICE TO LOS ANGELES, SAN FRANCISCO, DENVER, PHOENIX.

Only on TWA. Completely refurnished interiors on all our 707s. New seats, carpets, fabrics, colors, etc.

Only on TWA. The Twin Seat in 707 coach. If the plane's not full, it can be three across, two across or even a couch.

Only on TWA. A choice of 2 first-run movies on every movie flight. One for general audiences, one for mature (nominal charge for movies in coach).

Only on TWA. A choice of 3 international meals in coach, 5 in first class, with wines, champagnes, liqueurs, cheeses and desserts (nominal charge for alcoholic beverages in coach).

Call your travel agent or TWA.

Let's flashback to 1972, a very special year.

Was this the year you were born?

Was this the year you were married?

Whatever the reason, this book is a celebration of your year,

THE YEAR 1972.

Turn the pages to discover a book packed with fun-filled fabulous facts. We look at the people, the places, the politics and the pleasures that made 1972 unique and helped shape the world we know today.

So get your time-travel suit on, and enjoy this trip down memory lane, to rediscover what life was like, back in the year 1972.

1972 Family Life in the USA

Imagine if time-travel was a reality, and one fine morning you wake up to find yourself flashed back in time, back to the year 1972.

What would life be like for a typical family, in a typical town, somewhere in America?

Young family at a Californian rally, 1972.

Caught between the counterculture movement of the late '60s, and the Disco era of the mid-'70s, 1972 was a year looking for direction. We were fed-up with the ongoing Cold War and the draining war in Vietnam. We were ready for a new focus.

The hippie view of the world, with its emphasis on peace, love and nature, had focused our collective attention on the anti-war, anti-pollution, and anti-consumerism movements. In the summer of 1972, the Watergate scandal rocked the nation, reinforcing our rejection of our parents' old traditions and conservative values. Our distrust and disgust for authority and for the status quo increased further. Women, African Americans, LGBT communities and environmentalists ramped up the fight for recognition and equality.

In the ten years to 1972, the US population had increased by 11% to 213.3 million.[1] The Baby Boomers were now a large, vocal population of young adults. Birth rates and family sizes were falling, thanks to changing family values and readily available contraceptives.

Top left: Arriving at the *Erie Canal Soda Pop Festival*, 4th Sept 1972.

Above: Peace March to Kezar Stadium, San Francisco, CA. 22nd April 1972.

Left: Sorority sisters, early '70s.

The feminist movement ensured women were more educated and confident. At the same time, divorce rates were rising. An estimated 50% of couples who married in 1972 would end up divorced in future years.[2]

Levels of education across the board had increased—82% of teenagers graduated high school in 1972 (up from 69.5% ten years earlier).[3] A further 36% of 18 to 19-year-olds continued to a higher education institution.[4]

[1] worldometers.info/world-population/us-population/.
[2] nationalaffairs.com/publications/detail/the-evolution-of-divorce.
[3] nces.ed.gov/pubs2011/dropout08/tables.asp &
safeandcivilschools.com/research/graduation_rates.php.
[4] statista.com/statistics/236093/higher-education-enrollment-rates-by-age-group-us.

Advertisement

The little camera that takes big pictures.

It's the new Kodak pocket Instamatic camera, the one that takes big pictures.

It takes good, clear $3^1/_2 \times 4^1/_2$-inch snapshots. It uses a remarkable new Kodak color film and has a multi-element lens. Just drop the new little film cartridge in the Pocket, and shoot.

Five Pockets to look into. All but one with automatic exposure control. At your photo dealer's, from less than $28.

New Kodak pocket Instamatic camera.

Did you know that the term "generation gap" was coined by the Baby Boomers to describe the differences between their attitudes and values, and those of their old-world parents? This new generation questioned everything about "the American Dream", even mixing their social and political views into their music and art.

A family portrait, 1970.

Universities and colleges became breeding grounds for free-thinking, liberal theories. Students often shared accommodation, partly for convenience and cost savings, but also to express a new way of living, cohabiting, exploring sexual freedoms and spiritual fulfillment.

College students on campus, 1971.

In 1972 the median family income was $11,120 a year.[1] Unemployment stood at 5.2%, with GDP growth at 5.3%.[2]

Average costs in 1972 [3]	
New house	$27,299
New car	$3,760
Washing machine	$170
Refrigerator	$290
A gallon of gasoline	$0.36

[1] census.gov/library/publications/1973/demo/p60-90.html.
[2] thebalance.com/unemployment-rate-by-year-3305506.
[3] thepeoplehistory.com and mclib.info/reference/local-history-genealogy/historic-prices/.

Life in the United Kingdom

Now just imagine you flashed back to a town in 1972 England. Although not all doom and gloom, the United Kingdom had found itself slipping on the world stage as America and the USSR battled for domination.

London had reigned as the center of global culture during the decade of the '60s, but by the '70s the shine had faded. The joyful, carefree optimism of England's Swinging Sixties could not last forever. The sentiment on the streets had shifted from frivolity to revolution. This attitude was echoed in the fashion, music, art and culture of the time.

London street scenes from 1972.

The "Troubles" in Northern Ireland peaked with the *Bloody Sunday* killings in January, and the *Bloody Friday* bombings in July. Nationalist campaigns became increasingly violent, spilling into the streets of cities across the UK as activists took to bombing commercial and political targets.

The British feminist movement had a long established history and continued to gain strength throughout the 1970s. The newly formed Women's Liberation Movement quickly grew to become a national movement, with thousands of grassroots groups. Their list of equal rights demands included equal pay, equal education, and free contraception.

The first Women's Liberation Movement protest march, 8th March 1971.

In 1972 the average age of marriage for women was 26, and the average age for the birth of their first child was 27.[1] The fertility rate was 2.2 births per woman, down from a peak of 2.9 in 1964.[2] The contraceptive pill (available since 1961) and the legalization of abortion in 1967 aided in this decline.

The Divorce Reform Act came into effect in 1971, allowing for divorce without reason and leading to a steep increase in divorce rates, beginning as early as 1972.

In the early '70s around 50% of families owned a car.[3] Within the larger cities, most people still relied on public transport.

10% of homes did not have internal toilets, while 9% were still without baths. 58% lacked telephones and 63% lacked central heating.[4]

Only 33% of 18-year-olds finished high school, a figure far lower than most other industrialized nations.

[1&2] ons.gov.uk/peoplepopulationandcommunity.
[3&4] ons.gov.uk/ons/rel/ghs/general-lifestyle-survey/2011/rpt-40-years.html.

Advertisement

No matter how much you use it, it's never used up.

Half the presents under the Christmas tree will be eaten, drunk, worn out or broken by New Year's Day. A notable exception is the Encyclopedia Americana–the present that never grows old.

In the years to come, scarcely a day will go by that some member of the family doesn't consult the Americana for authentic, accurate information always available at your fingertips.

And besides a bag full of facts, he'll find Americana to be a book full of absorbing reading. It's the quality of the writing that makes our 30-volume set such a good book.

Written by writer-experts who know how to make a page come alive, Encyclopedia Americana is hard to put down.

Cash price $375.00 plus handling and shipping. Budget terms available.

By 1972, the UK was nearly half-way through repaying its post-war debt to America and Canada. The 20-year post-war building boom, which had kept cash flowing and unemployment low, was over.

Economic growth in the UK was only half that of Germany and Japan, with annual GDP having slipped from 2nd place in 1960 (behind only USA), to 5th place in 1972. Moreover, UK GDP per capita had fallen to 25th place in world rankings.[1]

By 1972, most of the former colonies of the United Kingdom had been granted independence. The cost for the UK to keep and defend them had proven too heavy a burden.

Across the nation, marches, protests, riots, strikes, and industrial strife were increasing. Inflation was also on the rise. The UK in 1972 was a country in decline. And this was just the beginning. The worse was yet to come.

Above: London's first *Gay Pride* march, 1st July 1972. The heavily policed event from Hyde Park to Trafalgar Square was focused more on awareness and activism than the festival atmosphere of today's events.

The remainder of the decade would bring a mounting series of economic crises, industrial actions and major political battles.

Engineering workers' strike at Tower Hill, London, 1st March 1973.

[1] nationmaster.com/country-info/stats/Economy/GDP.

Rise of the Communes

Late 1960s–Mid-1970s

By the early '70s, the Baby Boomers were young adults. Everything about them was a break-away from their parents: their music, their fashion, their values, their personal and sexual freedoms. They were non-traditional, non-conformist, anti-authority, anti-consumerist, anti-war, politically active, experimental drug users, hippies, believers and disbelievers. Anything was possible. Everything was acceptable.

The "Back to the Land" movement and the rise of communal living in the late '60s and early '70s were lifestyle expressions of freedom of choice. Communes were anti-establishment and experimental, communes were whatever the inhabitants chose them to be. Up to 3000 communes existed in the USA during this period.[1]

In the state of Vermont, a haven for hippies, an estimated one third of young adults (below age 34) were living communally.[2]

[1&2] forbes.com/sites/russellflannery/2021/04/11/what-happened-to-americas-communes/?sh=7454bc05c577

Most communes encouraged co-ownership of possessions, collective chores and shared child-raising. For many, clothes, monogamy and drug usage were optional. By rejecting the 40-hour work week, many communards stamps, or temporary odd jobs to keep themselves nourished.

In rural areas communards practiced living off the land, setting up farms, building their own houses and selling handicrafts.

Myrtle Hill Farm, Vermont.

A geodesic dome house built at Myrtle Hill Farm, Vermont. Recalls one communard, "In 1971 a young man named Bernie Sanders visited Myrtle Hill Farm... Sanders' tendency to just sit around talking politics and avoid actual physical labor got him the boot."[1]

Communards at Hog Farm,

The rise of communal living in the late '60s and early '70s was worldwide. Although the vast majority only survived a few years, some communes continue to exist today.

[1] From *We Are As Gods: Back to the Land in the 1970s on the Quest for a New America* by Brian Doherty.

Advertisement

Now you can get 4-4-2 four great ways. And that includes a new, low-priced way! (You're welcome.)

How can we do it? Easy. We've come up with a great new 4-4-2 Sport/Handling Package. And you can order it on four Cutlass models–the Cutlass Supreme Convert, way back there. The Cutlass Hardtop and Cutlass S Coupe, next in line. And that gorgeous Cutlass S Hardtop, front and center. All different. All great.

Here's what the 4-4-2 Package includes: FE2 suspension with heavy-duty front and rear stabilizer bars; wide 14x7" wheels; louvered hood; special 4-4-2 grille; hood and body paint stripes; 4-4-2 identification. And you can order a Hurst Competition Shifter, if you like.

Engine choice? That's a whole new ballgame, too! A spirited 350-cube 2-barrel V-8 is standard. But you can order a 350 4-barrel. Or a 455-cubic incher with 4-barrels, flared dual exhaust outlets, and a specially sculptured rear bumper. Or order our top package, the W-30 with a dual-intake fiberglass hood and a factory-blueprinted 455 Cold-Air V-8!

The point is this: Now you can "pack up" and go 4-4-2 in more ways than ever. And you can do it for less! Go do so–at your nearest Olds dealer's.

Our Love Affair with Automobiles

Our love affair with automobiles began back in the early '50s, and by 1972 America's car addiction was unrivaled in the world. More than 96.5 million cars traveled our roads. Vehicle numbers had risen 47% during the preceding 10 years. Although automobile costs had risen markedly, so too had real wages, making cars increasingly affordable. The family car had become a necessity we could not survive without.

Americans purchased 10.94 million cars in 1972, setting a new record.

Increased car ownership and the creation of the National Highway System gave us a new sense of freedom. Office commuters could live further out from city centers, in cleaner and more spacious suburban developments, and commute quickly and comfortably to work.

Rural areas faced a steady decline as the suburban population continued to rise. By the early 1970s, only 26% of the population remained in rural areas.

Traffic congestion in Atlanta, 1972.

SouthPark Mall in Charlotte, North Carolina, 1971.

Catering to the suburban lifestyle, fully enclosed, air-conditioned shopping malls sprang up nationwide. A typical design saw one or two anchor stores with hundreds of smaller specialty shops, sitting within a vast expanse of carparks.

Detroit was the car manufacturing powerhouse of America, where "the Big Three" (Ford, General Motors and Chrysler) produced the bulk of cars sold. Although still renowned for their gas-guzzling "muscle cars", pressure from imports and domestic demand for more compact, fuel-efficient cars led to a general downsizing. Compact and sub-compact car sales grew, increasing markedly after the Arab embargo oil crisis of 1973.

American muscle cars increasingly battled to maintain relevance and dominance. These high-performance coupes with large, powerful V-8 engines and rear-wheel drive had been designed to satisfy our desire for power above all else. But the introduction of the Clean Air Act of 1970 forced automakers to drastically reduce emission pollutants. Clean air equipment became the new focus, robbing engines of much of their raw power and performance.

American auto makers responded to the stricter federal requirements, and to the increased competition from imports, by creating compact, more fuel-efficient car models. However poor design, inadequate engineering and manufacturing led to a stream of disasters, damaging the customer experience.

Five car-producing countries dominated the industry in 1972: Japan, Germany, England, and France, with America in the top spot. Japan's meteoric rise into this elite group had been particularly aggressive, and their cars stood poised to dominate the world markets.

Japanese cars were reliable, affordable, compact, efficient and popular, quickly making Toyota, Nissan, Mitsubishi, Mazda, Datsun, and Honda the export market leaders. Japanese car exports increased nearly 200-fold from start to end of the '60s.

As we became more aware of the hidden dangers and impracticalities inherent in American car designs, German and Japanese cars were seen as more reliable, safer and more fuel-efficient.

17th Feb– Volkswagen's Beetle became the world's best-selling car, breaking the four-decade long record held by Ford's Model T.

Advertisement

Do people own Cadillacs because they get more out of life, or...

do people get more out of life because they own Cadillacs? It's hard to say. Because Cadillacs have been such an integral part of the good life for 70 years now. In prestige, in performance, in pure driving pleasure, probably nothing offers more deep-seated satisfaction than owning a Cadillac. Perhaps no other automobile receives such universal admiration and respect. Or can contribute more to your driving peace of mind. Small wonder then that Cadillac resale value is traditionally the highest of any car built in the land. You could say that the only question remaining is: Do you want to visit your authorized Cadillac dealer today... or tomorrow?

There's no question about this. Real progress is being made by Cadillac and others in the massive effort to remove the automobile from the air pollution problem. You can help by using no-lead or low-lead fuels. Getting a tune-up regularly. Having the emission control systems on your car checked often. Thank you, Cadillac Motor Car Division.

Advertisement

You don't sail a boat just to get across the water. The fun is in the doing. The pleasure of motion under control. Mustang drivers understand that. If all they wanted was to get from here to there, they'd be driving something else. Not a Ford Mustang.

With independent front suspension and an anti-sway bar to give you good control, good road handling. With bucket seats to position you comfortably behind the wheel. With a cockpit design and floor mounted shift that give you a beautiful feeling the instant you're inside.

There are five sporty Mustang models: Hardtop, SportsRoof, Convertible, Mach 1, Grandé. And a selection of five engines, three transmissions. What it takes to make driving a beautiful experience is what Ford puts into Mustang.

Clean Air for All

Driver wearing a smog mask in the early '70s, Los Angeles, USA.

Our love affair with gas-guzzling, pollutant-emitting cars caused our air quality to deteriorate to severely unhealthy levels throughout the '50s and '60s. By the early '70s, pollutants from exhaust and industries left major cities regularly blanketed in a hazardous thick brown haze.

By 1972, the Clean Air Act (passed 31st December 1970) had become a serious concern for car manufacturers. The Act required leaded petrol engines to be phased out, and new vehicles to be engineered for cleaner emissions and fuel efficiency.

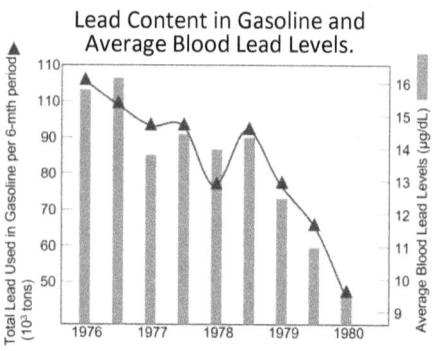

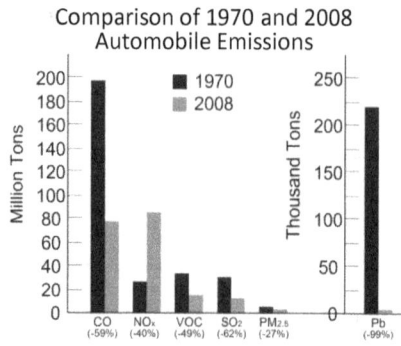

The Act required a 90% reduction of emissions from new automobiles within five years, targeting six major public health pollutants, including lead and carbon monoxide.

The US Environmental Protection Agency gave the states a short five years to meet these clean air quality goals, forcing the states to put pressure on industry and vehicle manufacturers.

The UK implemented their first Clean Air Act in 1956. Their revised Act of 1970 specifically targeted carbon monoxide and hydrocarbons from automobile engines.

In Canada, Australia, and across Europe, similar legislations were developed throughout the '70s to tackle the undeniable problem of automobile-created photochemical smog which affected all major cities.

Different countries set their own standards, some more stringent than others. They also created their own methods for emissions testing of vehicles prior to sale, and of air quality testing for cities.

New York aerial view in 1973 and now.

L.A. Grand Avenue in 1967 and now.

London's Great Fog of 1952 resulted in the deaths of 12,000 Londoners.

Advertisement

How to get more out of your appliances and save gas, too.

You'll find gas appliances are unusually dependable and easy to care for. Here are a few suggestions to keep them running at top efficiency and help save our country's energy supply.

The gas range. It should burn with a steady blue flame. If it's yellow, your burners could be clogged. Just lift them out and wash them. If that doesn't do it, call a serviceman and have them adjusted. Another gas saver —the automatic controls on today's new gas ranges.

The furnace. To get it ready for the winter, call your dealer or heating contractor. He'll lubricate the motor, check the controls, be sure it's in top working order. In a warm-air system, change the filters at least once a year. You save gas when your furnace works efficiently.

The gas water heater. There's practically no maintenance with a gas water heater. The important thing is to have one big enough for your whole family. Modern gas water heaters save on gas because they have new, well-insulated linings that help keep the water hot.

The gas dryer. Don't overload it—and after every load clean out the lint filter. Your owner's manual shows you where it's located on your dryer. You'll save gas and have gentle drying year after year. In most areas, gas gives you five loads for the price of one in any other dryer.

Gas, clean energy for today and tomorrow 🔥
AMERICAN GAS ASSOCIATION

How to get more out of your appliances and save gas, too.

You'll find gas appliances are unusually dependable and easy to care for. Here are a few suggestions to keep them running at top efficiency and help save our country's energy supply.

The gas range. It should burn with a steady blue flame. If it's yellow, your burners could be clogged. Just lift them out and wash them. If that doesn't do it, call a serviceman and have them adjusted. Another gas saver—the automatic controls on today's new gas ranges.

The furnace. To get it ready for the winter, call your dealer or heating contractor. He'll lubricate the motor, check the controls, be sure it's in top working order. In a warm-air system, change the filters at least once a year. You save gas when your furnace works efficiently.

The gas water heater. There's practically no maintenance with a gas water heater. The important thing is to have one big enough for your whole family. Modern gas water heaters save on gas because they have new, well insulated linings that help keep the water hot.

The gas dryer. Don't overload it—and after every load clean out the lint filter. Your owner's manual shows you where it's located on your dryer. You'll save gas and have gentle drying year after year. In most areas, gas gives you five loads for the price of one in any other dryer.

Nuclear Bomb Testing

Remember when dropping nuclear bombs was commonplace? For more than 40 years, the Nuclear Arms Race gave the USA and USSR the pretext needed to test nuclear bombs on a massive scale. Nearly 1,700 bombs were dropped by the superpowers, most of them during '60s and '70s. A further 300 were tested by China, France, and the UK. These tests served to understand the effectiveness and capacity of each bomb type. They also acted as a deterrent to enemy nations.

Underwater nuclear test at Bikini Atoll. In 1963 the two superpowers signed a Nuclear Test Ban treaty, limiting tests to underground only. Space, atmospheric, and underwater tests would cease.

During 1972, the US carried out 27 nuclear tests, mostly at the Nevada Proving Grounds, while USSR tested 24 nuclear bombs.

The UK, France and China were also testing their nuclear arsenal, though not at the same intensity.

Pakistan secretly began a nuclear weapons program, in response to the threat of nuclear weapons already being developed by India.

US troops and observers witness the detonation of *Small Boy* at the Nevada Proving Grounds in 1962, (prior to the Test Ban).

Although most of the test sites were largely uninhabited by humans, some of them were densely populated. The effects of radioactive fallout plagued local populations for years afterwards.

Battlefield Vietnam

We had long ago grown tired and fed-up with the ongoing Vietnam War (known in Vietnam as the American War). US troops in Vietnam had dropped from a peak of 536,100 in 1968, to just 133,200 by the start of 1972. The reduction in numbers came as President Nixon revealed, on 25th Jan 1972, that his National Security Adviser, Henry Kissinger, had been secretly negotiating a peace plan with the North Vietnamese for more than two years.

US military help South Vietnamese army to flee. Battle of An Loc. Easter Offensive, April 1972.

Children play on a destroyed tank in Kontum, South Vietnam, Dec 1972.

Meanwhile US troops continued their bombing campaigns in North Vietnam unabated. The heaviest bombing since the commencement of the war was carried out 8th-13th February. Bombing intensified further in April during an Easter Offensive, even while Kissinger was in Moscow negotiating with the Russians.

By year's end, numbers would fall to 24,200,[1] and three months into the new year, President Nixon would bring the last men home. It would bring an end to America's involvement in Vietnam's 30-year-long bloody civil war. What had started as a commitment by the USA to help South Vietnam expel its northern invaders, and prevent the spread of communism, seemed so much less important now.

[1] americanwarlibrary.com/vietnam/vwatl.htm.

Anti-Vietnam War Sentiment

1955–1975

Anti-war sentiment had been escalating for many years, as more and more protestors took to the streets against what they believed to be an immoral war.

Numerous anti-war marches and civil disobedience campaigns were waged throughout the months of April and May, culminating with a 100,000 strong march on 22nd April 1972 in New York. At the same time, people gathered in cities across the USA and around the world.

Anti-war peace march in San Francisco, CA. 22nd April 1972.

In July, actress Jane Fonda, the war's most high-profile critic, traveled to North Vietnam. She would speak on Hanoi Radio. Her outspoken activism earned her the nickname "Hanoi Jane".

Forced to fight a war they didn't believe in, morale among the draftees was low. Drug usage became rampant. It is estimated up to 50% of American soldiers experimented with marijuana, opium and heroin, cheaply available on the streets of Saigon. American military hospitals would later report drug abuse victims far outnumbered actual war casualties.

Watergate–Scandal in the White House 17th June 1972

It was the scandal that brought down a president, and forever scarred American politics. In May 1972, members of President Nixon's re-election committee broke into the Democratic National Committee's headquarters in the Watergate building, stole documents and bugged the telephones. When the wiretaps failed to work properly, five men returned on 17th June to try again. Thanks to a vigilant security officer, they were arrested as they entered the building.

Watergate newspaper headlines from the '70s.

The President vehemently denied having links to the "burglars", while secretly paying hush money to cover-up the crimes, and instructing the CIA to obstruct an FBI investigation. The public believed his lies, handing him another landslide re-election victory.

Meanwhile a whistle-blower known as *Deep Throat* provided *Washington Post* reporters Bob Woodward and Carl Bernstein damning proof of the illegal espionage. As Nixon's aides began to turn against him, the House Judiciary Committee voted to impeach the President for obstruction of justice, contempt of Congress, and abuse of power. Nixon resigned in August 1974. His crimes were quickly pardoned by his successor, President Gerald Ford.

Movies about Watergate: *All the Presidents Men* (Warner Bros. 1976), *The Post* (20th Century Fox, 2017).

Advertisement

United States Air Force
Make your first love last a lifetime.

Art Edwardson fell in love at the age of 6½. In his mind he still sees her. A vision of metallic beauty, poised on the runway, waiting to take off. Art held on to his young love through high school, until the Air Force made his boyhood dream a reality. A dream he lived out as a pilot in the Air Force. Today Art is a pilot for one of the world's largest airlines. His story is the perfect example of an Air Force specialty... the re-usable skill.

Two kinds of people find themselves in the Air Force: those who know exactly who they are and what they want and those who are still searching. Those who know just need opportunity. For the rest the Air Force uses aptitude tests, psychological interviews and good old common sense to help find the one job among hundreds they'll do best. Either way–Air Force training gives a man a skill he can always carry with him... even back to civilian life.

The product of the Air Force's training programs are skilled technicians. They represent a substantial natural resource for the whole nation. The jobs we train America's youth for are needed not only by the Air Force, but also by the civilian job market. In fact, each year over $300 million worth of Air Force investment in trained manpower is returned to civilian economy. Remember. The re-usable skill... it's an Air Force specialty.

Troubles in Northern Ireland-Bloody Sunday

1972 is officially the deadliest year on record for the 30-year-long nationalist campaign in Northern Ireland, known as *The Troubles*. Almost 500 people were killed as Roman Catholic Republicans (IRA) fought against Protestant Ulster Unionists and the British military. Although often mistaken for a war of religion, *The Troubles* was in fact a political war. The Republicans were fighting for the reunification of Northern Ireland with the Republic of Ireland. The Unionists were determined to keep Northern Ireland as part of the United Kingdom.

British Troops arrest a suspected Republican on the first day of *Internment* (imprisonment without trial), 9th Aug 1971.

An injured woman is comforted by a British soldier in the aftermath of an IRA bomb blast in Donegall Street, Belfast. 20th March 1972.

The Troubles flared up in the late '60s with British troops arriving to quell the violence. The troops remained, patrolling Northern Ireland's streets for 37 years. Although their role was officially to be neutral peace-keepers, they were permitted to imprison IRA suspects without trial, and were widely condemned for covertly supporting the Unionists.

A section of Peace Wall.

Peace Walls were hastily erected throughout the cities and suburbs of Northern Ireland, physically separating Republicans from Unionist neighborhoods.

A total of 34 km (21 miles) of Peace Walls were built by the British Government, which in recent years have become something of a tourist attraction.

30th Jan– The *Bloody Sunday* massacre in Derry, Northern Ireland, sparked the deadliest year for *The Troubles*. British troops, in full view of the public and press, attacked and shot at unarmed protestors. Fourteen civilians died and countless were injured. The sheer brutality of the attack generated waves of anti-British rioting across Ireland and England, boosting membership, finance and sympathy for the IRA.

Within one week the British Embassy in Dublin, Ireland, was burned to the ground. IRA guerrilla-style bombing campaigns intensified against British infrastructure, commercial and political targets. Unionists attacked the wider Catholic community in "retaliation". A secret British Army unit, the Military Reaction Force, carried out undercover drive-by shootings against unarmed Catholic civilians. Hardly a day passed without a bombing or shooting attack somewhere.

Above and below: *Bloody Sunday*, 30th Jan 1972. The British Army faced off against protesters in Derry, Northern Ireland.

28th Mar– The escalating violence caused the British government to suspend the Parliament of Northern Ireland and impose direct rule from London.

13th Jul– British troops stormed in and wrested control of the IRA's "no-go" strongholds.

21st Jul– The *Bloody Friday* attacks followed ten days of bombings and fierce daily gun battles between the IRA and British troops. Twenty large IRA bombs exploded simultaneously around Belfast. No warnings were given.

20,000 British troops remained in Northern Ireland at the end of 1972.

UK Miner's and Docker's Strikes

1972 recorded an unprecedented level of strike days, not seen since the General Strikes of 1926. Building workers, steel workers, car assembly workers, miners and dockers all walked off the job demanding change.

For six weeks in January and February, coal mines across the UK came to a standstill as British miners staged a national strike, their first in nearly 50 years. Demanding better pay on par with other industries, the miners were soon joined by railway workers and power station workers who agreed not to handle coal in solidarity.

As electricity supply struggled to keep up with the winter demand, a state of emergency was declared on 9th February. Many homes and businesses were without power for up to nine hours a day as electricity was rationed on a rotational basis. Pubs, shops, and other businesses operated by candlelight.

Millions were laid-off as business struggled to stay operational. A pay deal was finally reached between the National Union of Mineworkers and the government, allowing miners to return to work on 28th Feb.

Strikes also rocked the docks as dockers railed against the new planned *Industrial Relations Act* which would permit forced redundancies. They opposed the use of shipping containers as these could be craned on and off ports, replacing manual labor.

Pentonville Five docker Vic Turner after his prison release.

In July, five picketing stewards landed in Pentonville Prison, raising awareness of the unjust new Act. Hundreds of thousands joined in the strikes, and as the country veered towards a General Strike, the new Act was abandoned and the "Pentonville Five" released.

Advertisement

The phone company wants more executives like Walt Chambers.

Walt Chambers is an Area Commercial Manager for the New Jersey Bell Telephone Company. He is responsible for fourteen telephone business offices handling 350,000 accounts in his home town of Newark and in suburban Essex County.

With the phone company since 1964, Walt has risen fast. "At New Jersey Bell," he says, "we are firmly committed to the practice that all of our employees compete on an equal basis. Our men and women are evaluated and are given chances for advancement or transfer on an equal basis."

And that's the way Walt intends to keep it for the 550 employees he supervises.

That's also the way we want it throughout the Bell System. At whatever level employees enter the company, we want them to do what they like to do and do best. So when openings exist, local Bell Companies are offering applicants and present employees jobs they may not have thought about before.

That's why we have women stringing telephone lines and men working as operators and service representatives.

AT&T and your local Bell Company are equal opportunity employers.

Advertisement

Start fresh with the right touch of menthol.
Belair

A refreshing offer:
   That Ross AM/FM portable radio they are enjoying can be yours. It's just one of over a thousand gifts you get free for Raleigh coupons, the valuable extra found on every pack of Belair.
   For your free copy of our Gift Catalog, write Box 12, Louisville, KY. 40201.

Australian PM Whitlam Dismissed

2nd December 1972

On 2nd December, Gough Whitlam led Australia's Labor Party to victory, breaking a 23-year hold by the outgoing conservative Liberal-Country Party. Many of the rights Australians now take for granted can be traced to the controversial social reforms of Whitlam's short three years in office.

Whitlam faces questioning after his dismissal, 11th Nov 1975.

Whitlam wasted no time implementing several major policy changes. During his first month in power, he brought home the last military advisers from Vietnam. He abolished conscription and released all conscientious objectors from jail.

He established the Department of Aboriginal Affairs and announced a royal commission into Aboriginal land rights, paving the way for the return of sacred lands to their indigenous owners.

Whitlam introduced free legal aid, free university education, and universal healthcare. He ratified the Racial Discrimination Act, and the Family Law Act, bringing no-fault divorce into law.

He replaced *God Save the Queen* with *Advance Australia Fair* as the national anthem of Australia.

Internationally, he reopened the Australian Embassy in Beijing. He also visited China, paving the way for other western leaders, and for future economic ties between Australia and China.

Whitlam in China, Nov 1973.

Whitlam won a second term in a 1974 snap election, before becoming the first and only Australian Prime Minister to be dismissed by the Governor-General, a controversial decision brought about by the 1975 constitutional crisis.

Summer Olympics 1972

26th Aug-12th Sep 1972

The Games of the XX Olympiad (Summer Olympics 1972) returned to Germany for the first time since the controversial Summer Games of 1936 in Berlin, where Adolf Hitler had banned Jewish athletes. Hitler had used the 1936 Games to showcase his Nazi ideal of Aryan supremacy.

In 1972, Germany was determined to present itself as an inclusive, peaceful, modern and democratic nation. A record 7,134 athletes participated in 195 events, making the Games the largest to date.

Unfortunately, the Games did not eventuate as their motto, *The Happy Games* (Die heiteren Spiele), projected.

Opening ceremony, Munich, 16th July '72.

The torch relay tradition began at the 1972 Munich Olympics. The torch's flame was provided by the Olympic fire, lit by the sun at the site of the ancient Olympics–the Temple of Hera in Olympia, Greece.

The torch was carried by 3,331 runners over 12 days, lighting the Munich Olympic cauldron to mark the start of the Games.

Over the years the torch relay has carried the flame on foot, on horseback, by boat, plane, train, canoe, camel, and more creatively, underwater and by laser beam.

Günter Zahn lights the cauldron in Munich.

Sporting highlights in Munich 1972 included 7 gold medals for USA's Mark Spitz in the pool, while Australia's Shane Gould won 5 medals. Olga Korbut, a young Soviet gymnast, won medals and our hearts, performing an astonishing backward release on the uneven parallel bars. The dangerous "Korbut flip" move has since been banned.

The USSR took home the most medals, winning 95 of them, followed by the USA, East Germany, then West Germany.

Massacre in Munich

5th-6th September 1972

Sadly, the harmony and unity of *The Happy Games* was tragically interrupted on the 9th day when five terrorists stormed the Olympic Village to ambush the Israeli team. Two athletes were killed while nine others were taken hostage. Their abductors were Black September extremists linked to the Palestinian group Fatah.

Eight men scaled the fence surrounding the Olympic Village at 4:30am on 5th September. Two Israeli team members were shot dead while trying to disarm the abductors. The terrorists demanded the release of more than 200 Palestinians from Israeli prisons.

After many hours of negotiations by phone, the nine hostages were blindfolded and taken by bus and helicopter to Fürstenfeldbruck Air Base to be flown to safety. West German police were waiting to ambush them, but the plan was badly thought through, and the abductors sensed the ruse.

The police, ill equipped and untrained for this mission, were forbidden from asking for military assistance. Lacking sniper rifles, they fired with assault rifles. The terrorists threw a hand grenade at the bound and gagged Israeli athletes, spraying the helicopters with bullets. All the athletes were killed, along with one policeman. Five of the terrorists lay dead. Another three were captured.

For the first time in Olympic history the games were suspended. 34 hours later, the IOC President declared, "The Games must go on!"

Top: Abductors on the balcony where the Israeli team were being held hostage, 5th Sept 1972.

Above: Coffins of the victims lined up in a Munich synagogue.

Below: Bombed remains of one of the helicopters carrying the Israeli athletes.

Operation Wrath of God   September 1972-1988

Less than two months after the massacre in Munich, Palestinian terrorists struck again—this time hijacking a Lufthansa passenger jet en route to Frankfurt. They demanded the release of the three Black September terrorists captured during the Olympic Games.

German authorities complied, releasing the men in exchange for the Lufthansa crew and passengers. The move was condemned by Israel, who accused Germany of "capitulating to terrorists".

The Israeli response was swift and lethal. Israel was no stranger to covert operations against Palestinian targets. With approval from Prime Minister Golda Meir, *Operation Wrath of God* was implemented, a covert assassination campaign aimed to track down and kill everyone involved the Munich massacre. With the help of their extensive spy network, a list comprising 25-30 Black September and PLO activists was drawn up.

Israeli Prime Minister Golda Meir at a press conference in Oct 1973.

Film poster for *Munich* (Universal Pictures, 23rd Dec 2005).

It is unknown how many people were directly killed by *Operation Wrath of God*. During the first 12 months, Palestinian operatives were gunned down or blown up in Rome, Paris, Cyprus, Lebanon, Athens, and Beirut.

Random killings, believed to be the work of Israeli spies, continued well into the 1980s.

In 2005, the film *Munich* was released. Starring Eric Bana and directed by Steven Speilberg, the plot followed a squad of *Operation Wrath of God* hitmen, as they track down and eliminate their targets.

Advertisement

THE 707 RE-BORN.

American Airlines new 707 LuxuryJet.

A wider, brighter, roomier look, inspired by our 747 and DC-10 LuxuryLiners.

A stand-up bar. Luxurious décor. Our sociable lounge.

American Airlines
Our passengers get the best of everything.

The 70 Re-born. American Airlines new 707 Luxury Jet.
- A wider, brighter, roomier look, inspired by our 747 and DC-10 Luxury Liners.
- A stand-up bar. • Luxurious décor. • Our sociable lounge.

It's something to see and you can only see it on American Airlines. If you've never flown in a 707 before you'll think it's beautiful. If you have, you'll be amazed. Inside everything looks wider, roomier, more spacious, yet the outside hasn't changed.

It's the 707 of the future, inspired by our wide-body Luxury Liners. And unlike our competitor who made just a few changes, we've ripped out the old interior completely, nose to tail.

Now the ceiling glows, the walls are sculptured, and the seats are the most modern in the industry. Coach passengers get the same legroom as first class passengers. And everybody gets more stand-up room, because the overhead "hat-rack" has been replaced by overhead compartments.

We've already started converting all of our 707s to beautiful 707 Luxury Jets. And since nobody else has even one, why fly any other airline?

American Airlines Our passengers get the best of everything.

Advertisement

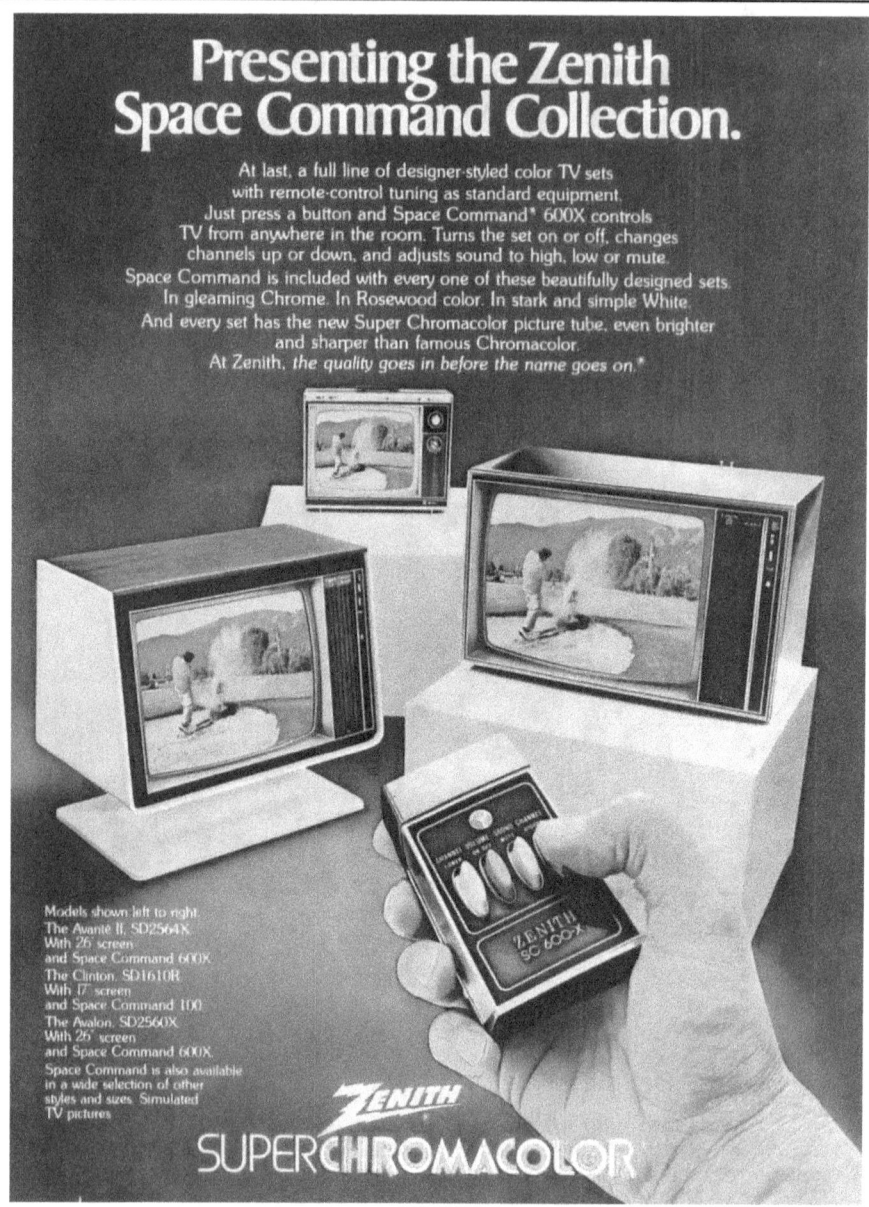

Presenting the Zenith Space Command Collection.

At last, a full line of designer-styled color TV sets with remote-control tuning as standard equipment. Just press a button and Space Command 600X controls TV from anywhere in the room. Turns the set on or off, changes channels up or down, and adjusts sound to high, low or mute. Space Command is included with every one of these beautifully designed sets. In gleaming Chrome. In Rosewood color. In stark and simple White. And every set has the new Super Chromacolor picture tube, even brighter and sharper than famous Chromacolor.

At Zenith, the quality goes in before the name goes on.

Grease Opens on Broadway   14th February 1972

The fictional Rydell High School of 1959 set the stage for one of our best loved stage and cinema musicals. *Grease* opened Off-Broadway at the Eden Theatre in Manhattan on 14th February, moving to Broadway's Broadhurst Theatre four months later.

The original 1972 Broadway cast of *Grease*.

The show ran until 1980 (3,388 performances), the longest run for any Broadway show at that time. Cast members from the original run included Patrick Swayze as Danny, John Travolta as Doody, and Richard Gere as Sonny. The '50s nostalgia, joyful plot, catchy songs and effervescent dance sequences provided a frivolous escape from our real-world drama.

The Broadway run was followed by productions in London's West End, with Richard Gere in the lead role as Danny. The show was produced in cities as far flung as Argentina, Australia, Spain, France, Mexico and South Africa. Touring casts also took the show across various countries for the enjoyment of smaller cities.

In 1978, Robert Stigwood adapted the stage show into a feature film, with John Travolta and Olivier Newton-John in the lead roles. The film and its soundtrack enjoyed major financial success. Reruns still delight audiences today.

Tuning in to Television

The television was our must-have appliance of the mid-20th century, taking pride of place in our family or living rooms. By 1972, nearly every US household owned a television,[1] with roughly half of them being color sets. Although color TVs had been around since the early '50s, and color broadcasts had become commonplace since the mid-'60s, the switch from black and white to color was very slow.

Outside the USA, some countries like Canada and the UK were catching up with color TV ownership and broadcasting. Australia, however, would wait till 1975 for its first color television broadcasts.

Elsewhere in the world, rates of television ownership lagged even further behind.

In many countries, television networks were government owned or subsidized, allowing for more focus on serious documentaries and news, without the constant concern of generating advertising revenue.

Carroll O'Connor and Mike Evans in *All in the Family* (CBS. 1971-1979).

Most Popular TV Shows of 1972 [3]

1. All in the Family
2. Sanford and Son
3. Hawaii Five-O
4. Maude
5. Bridget Loves Bernie
= The NBC Sunday Mystery Movie
7. The Mary Tyler Moore Show
= Gunsmoke
9. The Wonderful World of Disney
10. Ironside
11. Adam-12
12. The Flip Wilson Show
13. Marcus Welby, M.D.
14. Cannon
15. Here's Lucy
16. The Bob Newhart Show
17. Tuesday Movie of the Week
18. Monday Night Football
19. The Partridge Family
= The Waltons
= Medical Center

[1] americancentury.omeka.wlu.edu/items/show/136.
[2] tvobscurities.com/articles/color60s/.
[3] Nielsen Media Research 1972-'73 season of top-rated primetime television series in the USA.

Although sitcoms and variety programs remained popular in 1972, a new wave of intense TV dramas was keeping us glued to our television sets. A slew of police, detective, or medical themed primetime TV programs hit our screens in the late '60s, and we were hooked.

Seven of the twenty top-ranking TV series for 1972 were medical or crime themed programs, most lasting well into the decade.

Zulu, Jack Lord, James MacArthur and Kam Fong in *Hawaii Five-O* (CBS. 1968-1980).

Airing for an impressive 12 seasons, *Hawaii Five-O* was largely shot on location in Honolulu, Hawaii. It followed a special police task force fighting organized crime across the Hawaiian Islands.

The original series ended in 1980, making it the longest running TV crime show at that time. A 2010 remake, based on the original series, ran for ten seasons.

Robert Young starred as Marcus Welby, with James Brolin as his head-strong young assistant and Elena Verdugo as their nurse, in *Marcus Welby, M.D.* (ABC. 1969-1976).

Loretta Swit, Wayne Rogers, Alan Alda and McLean in *M*A*S*H* (CBS. 1972-1983).

Bill Daily, Marcia Wallace, Peter Bonerz, Bob Newhart, and Suzanne Pleshette in *The Bob Newhart Show* (CBS. 1972-1978).

The television networks were quick to turn out new programs to keep us tuning in. Here are a few of the new programs that aired for the first time in 1972: *M*A*S*H*, *The Bob Newhart Show*, *Emergency!*, *The Magic Garden*, *The Rookies*, *The Waltons*, and *WWF Championship Wrestling* (1972-86).

Richard Thomas and Ellen Corby in *The Waltons* (NBC. 1971-

Michael Ontkean, Sam Melville, Georg Stanford Brown, and Gerald S. O'Loughlin in *The Rookies* (ABC. 1972-1976).

Advertisement

Because you buy color TV for keeps...
we use more gold fillings than all the dentists in America.

Zenith's Gold Video Guard Tuner, the heart of the color TV system, has contact points of 16-karat gold. Why? Because gold contacts stay cleaner and last longer, to give you sharper reception and greater picture stability over the years.

Only Zenith makes TV tuners with gold contacts. And there are dozens of other examples of how Zenith goes all the way to build the finest TV set you can buy.

Even with this kind of dedication to quality, we know that occasionally some of you have problems with our products. And if that happens, you could care less about how good our reputation is. Over the years we have been proud of the strong relationship we have established between ourselves, our dealers, and you, the consumer. We are determined to keep your confidence. If a Zenith product doesn't live up to *your* expectations, let us hear from you. Write directly to the Vice President, Customer Relations, at Zenith Radio Corporation, 1900 North Austin Avenue, Chigago, Illinois 60639.

We want the opportunity to give your problems our personal attention.

At Zenith, we mean it when we say, *the quality goes in before the name goes on.*

1972 in Cinema and Film

As cinema-goers, our interests and focus had shifted away from traditional classic Hollywood standards, which were often bounding with optimism and happy endings. We were seeking movies that offered more depth, more pain and a sense of reality.

By 1972, a new breed of directors like Francis Ford Coppola, Martin Scorsese and Stanly Kubrik demanded more artistic control. They bravely tackled darker, more gritty, pessimistic themes of war, crime, depression and inner turmoil. The era of big cinema houses owning their actors and controlling their directors had ended.

Al Pacino in *The Godfather* (Paramount Pictures, 1972).

Harvey Keitel and Robert De Niro in *Mean Streets* (Warner Bros. 1973).

A new generation of brooding method-style actors rose to replace the retiring golden-era stars. Dustin Hoffman, Robert De Niro, Meryl Streep, Al Pacino, Jack Nicholson and Harvey Keitel are some of our enduring favorites.

1972 film debuts

Nick Nolte
Samuel L. Jackson
Ben Kingsley
Steve Martin
Jodie Foster
Lily Tomlin

Little Billy
Together for Days
Fear Is the Key
Another Nice Mess
Napoleon and Samantha
Scarecrow in a Garden of Cucumbers

Stanley Kubric received death threats for his disturbing, violent dystopian sci-fi *Clockwork Orange* (Warner Bros. Jan 1972). At his request, the film was withdrawn from British cinemas for 27 years.

* From en.wikipedia.org/wiki/1972_in_film.

Top Grossing Films of the Year

1	The Godfather	Paramount Pictures	$86,300,000
2	The Poseidon Adventure	20th Century Fox	$42,000,000
3	What's Up, Doc?	Warner Bros.	$28,000,000
4	Deliverance	Warner Bros.	$22,500,000
5	Jeremiah Johnson	Warner Bros.	$21,900,000
6	Cabaret	Allied Artists Pictures	$20,250,000
7	Deep Throat	Bryanston Distributing Co.	$20,000,000
8	The Getaway	National General Pictures	$18,000,000
9	Lady Sings the Blues	Paramount Pictures	$9,666,000
10	Everything You Always Wanted to Know About Sex	United Artists	$8,828,000

* From en.wikipedia.org/wiki/1972_in_film by box office gross in the USA.

The Godfather received critical acclaim, winning 3 Academy Awards from 7 nominations. It was for a while the highest grossing film ever made, propelling the careers of Al Pacino and director Francis Ford Coppola, and revitalizing the career of Marlon Brando. A 1974 sequel and 1990 epilogue completed the trilogy.

A Decade of Disasters

The Poseidon Adventure
(20th Century Fox, 1972).

The Towering Inferno
(20th Century Fox, 1974).

The decade of the '70s saw the disaster movie genre reign supreme at the box office. Large casts, multiple plot lines, life or death calamities and impossible tales of survival kept us on the edge of our seats.

Earthquake (Universal, 1974).

Tidalwave (Toho, 1973).

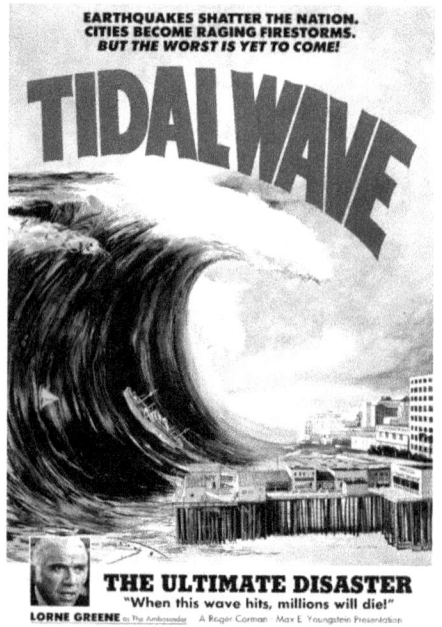

Advertisement

Maybe your next stereo should be 3 stereos.
 You can get them all in one trip if you bring home one Sony. The Sony HP-149A. Because it combines a stereo tuner/amplifier, a stereo record changer, and a stereo cassette recorder.
 The tuner/amplifier first. It's an all-solid-state FM stereo/FM-AM-Sony. Complete with the IF filters all Sony tuners have. For maximum sensitivity and selectivity. The record changer is a 4-speed BSR that stacks six at a time. With the all-solid-state Sony cassette recorder you can tape your own stereo right off either one, or live, using the optional Sony microphone.
 Tuner, changer, cassette, whichever of the three you're listening to, the wall-to-wall sound will be courtesy of a 2-way Sony speaker system. Each speaker features a $6^1/_2$-inch woofer and a 2-inch tweeter.
 The price for all this stereo is $239.95.* For a little less money you can get just as much stereo with a Sony HP-148A. It's sort of a sister set, with an 8-track stereo cartridge player instead of the stereo cassette player/recorder. Take away the cassette player and the cartridge player and you've still got a first-class Sony. The HP-140A.
 We wouldn't want you to buy more Sonys than you need.

Musical Memories

By 1972, the anti-war movement and musicians who had given us a voice were running out of steam. Summed up by Don McLean's chart-topping single, *American Pie* was an $8^1/_2$ -minute anthem to displaced youth. Our collective musical soul had lost direction.

AM radio continued to drive the singles charts, pushing feel-good artists like Donny Osmond, David Cassidy, Bread and the Carpenters. But other musicians were questioning AM's relevance as audiences increasingly tuned in to FM radio, where album cuts were broadcast.

Singer songwriters like Elton John, Cat Stevens, James Taylor, Joni Mitchel, and Carly Simon turned inward, exploring their emotions and anxieties. Alice Cooper and Pink Floyd reached out to the aimless and confused. The Rolling Stones released their seminal album *Exile on Mainstreet*.

Elton John in Hamburg, 1972.

Soul musicians were also carving their own paths, gaining artistic freedoms, and breaking down the racial divide through music. Stevie Wonder released two landmark albums in 1972, *Music of My Mind* and *Talking Book*.

Marvin Gaye's groundbreaking live recorded album *What's Going On Live* explored hatred, suffering, injustice, drug abuse and poverty from the viewpoint of a returning Vietnam Vet. It was a marked departure from the usual Motown sound.

In June and July, as The Rolling Stones continued their *American Tour 1972*, police battles and chaos plagued them at every stop. In Vancouver 31 policemen were injured, while in Montreal a bomb destroyed the band's equipment. In Arizona fans were met with tear gas. In San Diego 60 arrests were made due to disturbances, with 81 arrests in Houston and 61 arrests in Washington D.C.

Mick Jagger & Keith Richards on tour, 1972.

18th Jul– Mick Jagger and Keith Richards landed in jail in Rhode Island following an altercation with a photographer. 15,000 fans were waiting for them at Boston Garden. Fearing a riot, Boston Mayor Kevin White intervened to have the rock duo released, then walked onstage to beg the audience to remain calm. State troopers rushed the band to the arena and the show got underway after midnight.

22nd May– Australian singer Helen Reddy released her single *I Am Woman*, co-written with Ray Burton. The song would be adopted by the women's movement as its enduring unofficial anthem.

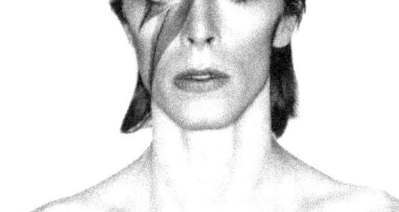

16th June– David Bowie transformed into his stage character *Ziggy Stardust*, an androgynous alien rock star visiting Earth to deliver a message of hope. Extravagant costumes and stage performances launched the mid-'70s Glam Rock genre.

1972 Billboard Top 30 Songs

	Artist	Song Title
1	Roberta Flack	The First Time Ever I Saw Your Face
2	Gilbert O'Sullivan	Alone Again (Naturally)
3	Don McLean	American Pie
4	Harry Nilsson	Without You
5	Sammy Davis Jr.	The Candy Man
6	Joe Tex	I Gotcha
7	Bill Withers	Lean on Me
8	Mac Davis	Baby, Don't Get Hooked on Me
9	Melanie	Brand New Key
10	Wayne Newton	Daddy Don't You Walk So Fast

Roberta Flack, 1976.

Sammy Davis Jr.

Don McLean, 1976.

Bill Withers, 1971.

	Artist	Song Title
11	Al Green	Let's Stay Together
12	Looking Glass	Brandy (You're a Fine Girl)
13	The Chi-Lites	Oh Girl
14	Gallery	Nice to Be with You
15	Chuck Berry	My Ding-a-Ling
16	Luther Ingram	(If Loving You Is Wrong) I Don't Want to Be Right
17	Neil Young	Heart of Gold
18	The Stylistics	Betcha by Golly, Wow
19	The Staple Singers	I'll Take You There
20	Michael Jackson	Ben

Neil Joung, 1970.

Neil Diamond, 1977.

	Artist	Song Title
21	Robert John	The Lion Sleeps Tonight
22	Billy Preston	Outa-Space
23	War	Slippin' into Darkness
24	The Hollies	Long Cool Woman in a Black Dress
25	Mouth & MacNeal	How Do You Do
26	Neil Diamond	Song Sung Blue
27	America	A Horse with No Name
28	Hot Butter	Popcorn
29	The Main Ingredient	Everybody Plays the Fool
30	Climax	Precious and Few

* From the *Billboard* top 30 singles of 1972.

Advertisement

Singin' in the rain.

Or heat. Or cold. Those are some of the things the TFM-8100W was made for. Because it's rubber sealed to resist moisture. It can even be knocked down by the wind. Because the heavy-duty, special plastic cabinet is unbreakable.

What's more, this 3-band (FM/AM/VHF weather, 162.55 mc) portable has the newly developed Sony Light Emitting Diode. It's an indicator, right in the tuning needle, that helps you tune the radio by brightening to red when a station is properly tuned.

There's a collapsible antenna. A shoulder strap. And a fine, rich sound (but that's nothing new for us).

So next time you plan to spend a lot of time outdoors, take the Sony all-weather portable along. And you'd better take a raincoat, just in case.

Nothing will happen to the radio. But we wouldn't want you to catch cold.

The Sony All-Weather Radio.

Advertisement

The gas grill that cooks your whole meal outdoors! Now you can cook out, roast out, smoke out, broil out, bake out, and chocolate cake out.

You can cook whole meals outdoors with Locke's Warm Morning Broilmaster II. It's a gas grill plus an oven. With two separate burners, two control knobs. Even an accessory smoker for southern-style slow smoking. Now anything you would have cooked in, you can cook out. It's so easy. No lighter fluids, no mess, no waiting. Gas reaches temperature fast so you're ready to cook in minutes. Gas, clean energy for today and tomorrow. See your Warm Morning dealer.

And here's our regular Broilmaster. It has redwood shelves, cool-touch handles, and enough cooking depth to rotisserie-broil a large turkey with the cover lowered. Portable model shown. Also available with set-in post or patio stand.

Fashion Trends of the 1970s

By the early '70s, the fashion industry had lost its way, with designers and consumers alike seeking new directions and answers to the changing times. This was a decade without guidance and without rules. Trends caught on and shifted quickly. Fashions were varied and experimental. Pants got wider, skirts got shorter, and boots got taller. And within a season the trends reversed. Anything was possible, everything was acceptable.

Walking down any street you would have found skirts worn mini, midi, or full length. Pants could be slim-fit, wide, or bell bottomed, hip-hugging or waist-clinching. Tops might be tie-dye swirl-patterned or bold solids. Shirts came long and loose, or tight and tailored.

Daywear pants-suit and skirt-suit.

Dresses came in all shapes and lengths too. They could be short Mod shifts, or calico lace prairie-style. They could be tailored with shirt-style collars and buttoned-down fronts. They could be long and loose caftans, flowing maxi-dresses, or waisted tailored-cut with belts and A-line skirts taken straight from the '50s.

Patchwork maxi-dresses
by Yves Saint Laurent.

The hippie and psychedelic fashions of the late '60s were adopted and modified by mainstream non-hippies into more elegant structured forms. Caftans, prairie dresses, patchwork fabrics, shawls, tassels and beads hit the runways, and the streets, in the early '70s.

Elizabeth Taylor during her bohemian period, 1969.   Maudie James models Thea Porter patchwork dress, 1970.   Weipert and Burda fashion show, 1972.

In contrast to the hippie trends, Mod dresses of the early '60s made a comeback. Space-age synthetics and plastics, widely used in the '60s, were replaced with comfortable cottons and stretch knits. In winter, tunic dresses could be worn over turtlenecks, with woolen stockings or thigh-high boots.

Mod mini dresses worn with white boots or shoes, early 1970s.

The '70s were the first full decade where pants for women gained mainstream acceptance, and we couldn't get enough of them. Pants could be worn for any occasion—pants-suits for the office, silky patterns for evenings, or blocks and geometrics dressed down for daywear. And let's not forget blue jeans, the staple of casual wear for both men and women.

Day wear pants from the Sears Spring/ Summer catalog, 1970.

In the early '70s men and women wore their pants gently flared at the base. As the decade progressed, the flares got wider and wider, exploding into bell-bottoms by the mid-'70s.

Embroidered denim.   Flared knit polyester pants.   Flared silky jumpsuits.

Advertisement

Times presents equal time for women.

Men don't have to wind watches anymore. Why should women?
The Ladies Electric TIMEX. There's no other watch quite like it in the world.
A beautiful way for a woman never to have to wind a watch again. A beautiful way to get electric accuracy.
In a whole fashion collection of styles so a lady can really have a choice.
The Ladies Electric TIMEX. It never needs winding. From $30.

Advertisement

Sears Give n Take II Stretch Jeans fit like you want jeans to fit. Comfortably. They look like you want jeans to look. Nice and new. And they feel like you want jeans to feel. Nice and old. All because they're made of a new 2-way stretch blend of Trevira® polyester, Avril® rayon and Lycra® spandex. Trim 'n Tight and Trim Regular models in patterned or solid flares.

What's more, they wear like you want jeans to wear. Wash, tumble dry, ready to go.

That's a lot to get, but you don't pay a lot to get it. Give n Take II Stretch Jeans at most Sears, Roebuck and Co. stores or through the regular and Big and Tall catalogs.

Give n Take II Stretch Jeans and all that goes with them at THE JEANS JOINT in

Give n Take II Stretch Jeans.

These Sears jeans stretch... the better to fit you with.

SUPPLIER FOR THE U.S. OLYMPIC TEAM

Give n Take II Stretch Jeans.
These Sears jeans stretch... the better to fit you with.

Sears Give n Take II Stretch Jeans fit like you want jeans to fit. Comfortably. They look like you want jeans to look. Nice and new. And they feel like you want jeans to feel. Nice and old. All because they're made of a new 2-way stretch blend of Trevira polyester, Avril rayon and Lycra spandex. Trim 'n Tight and Trim Regular models in patterned or solid flares.

What's more, they wear like you want jeans to wear. Wash, tumble dry, ready to go.

That's a lot to get, but you don't pay a lot to get it. Give n Take II stretch Jeans at most Sears, Roebuck and Co. stores or through the regular and Big and Tall catalogs.

Give n Take II Stretch Jeans and all that goes with them at

THE JEANS JOINT in Sears *The Men's Store.*   Supplier for the U.S. Olympic Team.

Shiny polyester Nik Nik shirts.   Stretch polyester tops and flared pants.   Terry toweling jumpsuits.

Caught between the hippie and mod fashion extremes of the early '70s, the rest of us settled for easy-care. Whether it was casual, formal or business attire, being easy to wash and drip-dry dictated what we wore. Non-iron wool jersey knits and non-iron polyester were the material of choice for men and women throughout the '70s.

The '70s are often considered to be the decade that fashion forgot (or the decade of fashion that we would rather forget). And it's not hard to see why. Anything and everything became acceptable, no matter how outlandish or mismatched.

Here are some of our more questionable fashion decisions from the decade.

Shiny stretch polyester jumpsuits.   Denim on denim.   Stretch knit pantsuits.   Safari suits.

John Travolta in *Saturday Night Fever* (Paramount Pictures, 1977).

Dancer at Studio 54, New York.

And then there was disco.
It shone so brightly. It glittered so briefly.
And in a flash, it was gone.

Sporting silver lamé jumpsuits.

Dancers at Studio 54, New York.

Model wears sequined jumpsuit.

A good club soda is like a good woman: it won't quit on you.

The only thing better than a club soda that's full of life at the end of a party is a girl who's full of life at the end of a party.

But what a man probably knows about a woman (or vice versa), you might not know about club soda. Especially ours.

You see, Canada Dry Club Soda gets its life through a special process called pin-point carbonation. Which means an uncapped bottle of our bubbles will last for twelve, twenty-four, even forty-eight hours.

So next time you're having a party with an intimate acquaintance, or a few hundred friends, mix your scotch or whiskey with Canada Dry Club Soda.

It may not do wonders for your love life. But it can do wonders for your drink.

Canada Dry: club soda with a long lasting bubble.

Advertisement

If you're one of those people who's a little bored with waking up to alarms, buzzers, disc jockeys and other people, Westclox has something for you.

It's our all new digital AM/FM clock radio with cassette recorder built right in. It does all the things a clock radio should do. And something a clock radio's never done. Because now, you can record your own voice on a cassette, pop it in the machine, set the timer, and nudge yourself gently out of bed the next morning.

Of course, you can also pre-record a favorite piece of music (which incidentally, can be taken right from the AM/FM radio) and have that wake you up.

The new Westclox AM/FM digital clock radio cassette recorder/player is finished in a rich walnut wood grain and sells for about $130.

The way we look at it, this radio gives you all the conventional ways of waking up in the morning.

And one very unconventional way.

Tomorrow morning wake up to the most beautiful sound you ever heard. You.

Also in Sports

3rd-13th Feb– Japan hosted the XI Olympic Winter Games in Sapporo, Hokkaido. With all new facilities constructed a full year in advance, Sapporo hosted an international sport week as a trial run in Jan 1971. The 1972 Games were a sporting and financial success for the city.

5th Feb– Bob Douglas became the 1st African American inducted to Basketball Hall of Fame. Douglas was the founder of the New York Renaissance (the Rens) basketball team from 1923-1949. He is known as the "Father of black professional basketball".

9th Apr & 18th Jun– Jack Nicklaus won the 36th Masters and the 72nd US Open. He is considered one of golf's greatest, having won 117 professional tournaments, including 18 majors, during his long career.

17th Apr– Eight women officially ran for the first time in the 74-year history of the Boston Marathon. It had previously been assumed the race would be too strenuous for women to finish. It would be another 12 years before women would run a marathon in the Olympics.

7th Jul & 9th Sep– America's Billie Jean King earned her 8th and 9th Grand Slam singles titles. She beat Australia's Evonne Goolagong 6-3, 6-3 at Wimbledon, then retained her US Open title, beating Australia's Kerry Melville Reid 6-3, 7-5. In 2006, the *USTA National Tennis Center* was renamed the *USTA Billie Jean King National Tennis Center* in her honor.

12th Aug– Australian cricketing brothers Ian and Greg Chappell both scored centuries in same Test Cricket innings. With their younger brother Trevor, the trio would ensure Australia's cricketing dominance throughout the '70s.

Advertisement

Puts Dad up front...

LA-Z-BOY® for Father's Day
ON SALE NOW!

Puts Dad up front... LA-Z-BOY for Father's Day ON SALE NOW!

Because your man is the greatest guy in the world, he deserves to be up front where the action is... in a La-Z-Boy Reclina-Rocker, the ideal television chair! He'll be able to enjoy any relaxing mood he wants. La-Z-Boy gives him the kind of comfort he deserves. You can put Dad's favorite reclining chair in your home and add beauty as well.

Mom, see your La-Z-Boy dealer today and discover true quality, comfort and beauty... and save during La-Z-Boy's Father Day Sale! Put Dad up front for Father's Day... where he belongs!

Technology and Medicine

2nd Mar– NASA launched the Pioneer 10 spacecraft, on a mission to the outer planets. Pioneer 10 became the first spacecraft from Earth to travel through the asteroid belt, and the first to pass-by Jupiter, transmitting data and images in December 1973.

19th Dec– Apollo 17, the sixth manned mission to the moon, returned to Earth concluding NASA's 9-year Apollo program. NASA would henceforth focus on the Space Shuttle Program, announced earlier in the year.

25th Jul– Jean Heller of the Associated Press exposed the *Tuskegee Experiment*–a 40-year medical study of 600 mostly poor and illiterate, African American sharecroppers from Tuskegee, Alabama. The US Public Health Service had recruited 399 men with syphilis, plus a further 201 as a control group, with promises of life-long medical treatment. The men were used as guinea pigs to research the progression of untreated syphilis, even though penicillin treatment had been available for 25 years.

29th Nov- Atari introduced Pong, the first commercially successful arcade video game. Magnavox Odyssey would sue Atari for patent infringement citing their similar 2D ping-pong game released earlier in the year. The two companies would revolutionize the market for at-home video games.

– Hamilton sold the first electronic digital wristwatch for $2,100.

– Polaroid introduced its first instant camera. The Polaroid SX-70 retailed for $180, excluding photo paper.

– Godfrey Hounsfield and Dr. Allan Cormack developed the first CT Scanner for EMI Laboratories in England, for which they would be jointly awarded the Nobel Prize in Physiology and Medicine in 1979.

– HBO (Home Box Office) launched the first pay-TV cable network, using domestic satellite transmission. By the end of the decade, nearly 16 million homes would subscribe to cable TV.

Other News from 1972

24th Jan– Japanese soldier Shoichi Yokoi was discovered in the jungles of Guam where he had been hiding for 28 years since WWII. He was repatriated to Japan, arriving home to a hero's welcome.

26th Jan– A bomb onboard Yugoslav Airlines Flight 367 exploded over East Germany killing 27 passengers and crew. 22-year-old Serbian flight attendant Vesna Vulovic fell 10,160m (33,330 ft) without a parachute and survived.

21st Feb– US President Richard M. Nixon arrived in China for an eight-day official visit, ending a 25-year diplomatic stand-off between the two nations.

US President Nixon shakes hands with Chinese Premier Zhou Enlai.

10th Apr– The Biological Weapons Convention, ensuring a total ban on the production, stockpiling, or transfer of biological weapons of war, was signed in London, Moscow and Washington, D.C. By 2013, 170 states had signed the agreement.

26th May– US President Nixon became the first US president to visit the Soviet Union since World War II, when he met with Soviet Premier Leonid Brezhnev in Moscow to sign the Anti-Ballistic Missile Treaty.

22nd May– The newly independent Republic of Sri Lanka (formerly the Dominion of Ceylon- a British colony) was born as its new constitution was ratified.

30th May– Three Japanese students, members of the Red Army Faction, arrived in Israel's Lod airport in Tel Aviv. Hired by the Popular Front for the Liberation of Palestine, the three attacked the crowd with sub-machine guns and hand grenades. 24 people were killed, including two of the attackers. A further 80 were injured.

4th Aug– General Idi Amin, self-appointed President of Uganda, ordered the expulsion of all 60,000 Asians from Uganda. He handed their business interests to his supporters, who lacked the management expertise to remain profitable. An estimated 300,000 people were killed during Amin's 8-year brutal dictatorship.

21st Sept– President Ferdinand E. Marcos declared Martial Law in the Philippines. His dictatorship lasted 14 years, by which time Marcos had amassed a great deal of personal wealth from criminal and corrupt activities. His exile in 1986 would reveal untold systematic human rights abuses, including torture, killings, and unjust incarcerations.

13th Oct– A Uruguayan plane carrying 45 passengers crashed in the Andes Mountains killing 12. Several survivors would succumb to the freezing temperatures, with 16 of them surviving 72 days. They were rescued after two of the survivors trekked for 12-days across the Andes by to find assistance.

7th Nov- Joe Biden won the US Senate election in Delaware. Eleven days later his wife and daughter were killed in a car accident.

Biden represented Delaware until 2009. He became US Vice-President (2009-2017), and the 46th President of the USA, inaugurated 20th January 2021.

Famous People Born in 1972

15th Jan– Claudia Winkleman, English television presenter & journalist.

16th Jan– Greg Page, Australian musician & actor (The Wiggles).

27th Jan– Guillermo Rodriguez, Mexican American TV personality.

5th Feb– Mary, Crown Princess of Denmark, born in Australia.

6th Mar– Shaquille O'Neal, American Basketball Hall of Fame center.

23rd Mar– Joe Calzaghe, Welsh boxer (10+ years super-middleweight world champion).

17th Apr– Jennifer Garner, American actress.

20th Apr– Carmen Electra (Tara Leigh Patrick), American model & actress.

25th Apr– Sara Baras, Spanish flamenco dancer & choreographer.

2nd May– Dwayne Johnson (The Rock), American pro wrestler, actor & producer.

2nd Jun– Wayne Brady, American actor, singer, comedian & TV personality.

2nd Jun– Wentworth Earl Miller III, American-British actor & screenwriter.

23rd Jun– Selma Blair, American actress.

23rd Jun– Zinédine Zidane, French soccer midfielder & Real Madrid manager.

10th Jul– Sofia Vergara, Colombian-American actress.

6th Aug– Geri Halliwell, British pop singer (Spice Girls).

15th Aug– Ben Affleck, American actor & director.

30th Aug– Cameron Diaz, American actress.

6th Sep– Idris Elba, English actor.

15th Sep– Jimmy Carr, English comedian.

15th Sep– Queen Letizia of Spain.

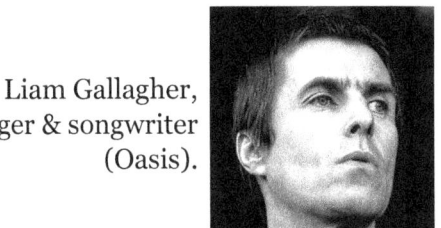

21st Sep– Liam Gallagher, British singer & songwriter (Oasis).

27th Sep– Gwyneth Paltrow, American actress.

28th Sep– Dita Von Teese, American burlesque artist.

17th Oct– Eminem (Marshall Bruce Mathers III), American rapper & actor.

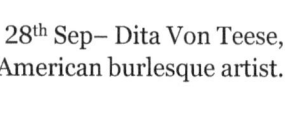

28th Oct– Brad Paisley, American country singer.

29th Oct– Gabrielle Union, American actress, author & activist.

31st Oct– Matt Dawson MBE, English rugby union halfback & broadcaster.

1st Nov– Toni Collette, Australian actress.

6th Nov– Thandiwe Newton, English actress.

14th Dec– Miranda Hart, English comedian & actress.

19th Dec– Alyssa Milano, American actress & activist.

29th Dec– Jude Law, English actor.

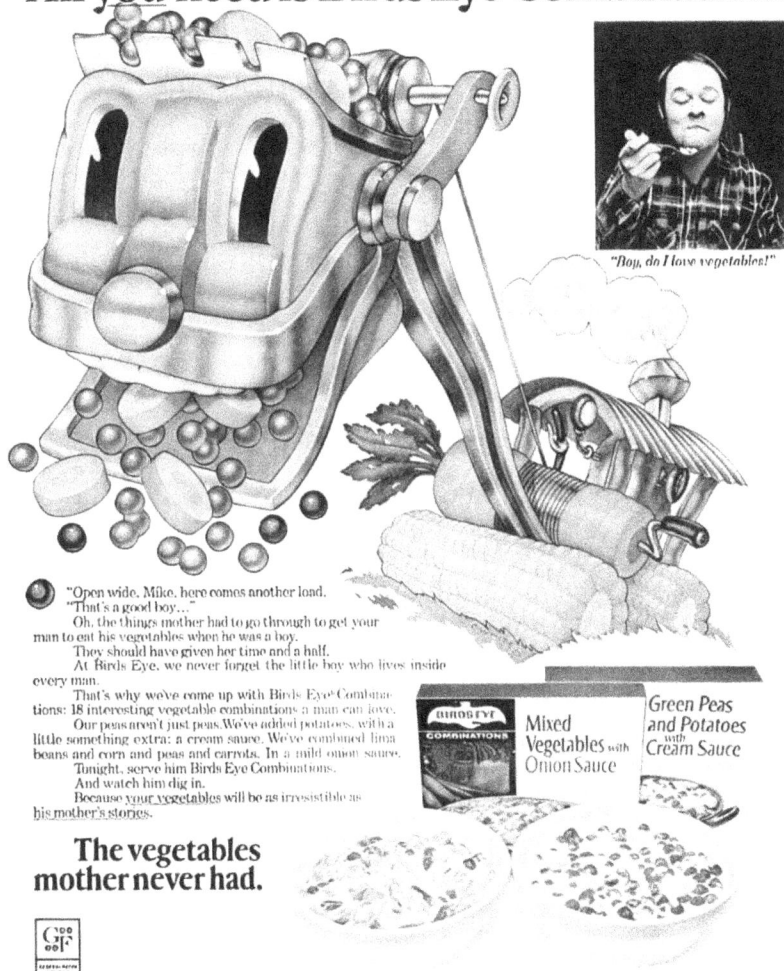

His mother needed a steam shovel. All you need is Birds Eye Combinations.
"Open wide, Mike, here comes another load."
"That's a good boy..."
Oh, the things mother had to go through to get your man to eat his vegetables when he was a boy.
They should have given her time and a half.
At Birds Eye, we never forget the little boy who lives inside every man.
That's why we've come up with Birds Eye Combinations: 18 interesting vegetable combinations a man can love.
Our peas aren't just peas. We've added potatoes, with a little something extra: a cream sauce. We've combined lima beans and corn and peas and carrots. In a mild onion sauce.
Tonight, serve him Birds Eye Combinations.
And watch him dig in.
Because your vegetables will be as irresistible as his mother's stories.
The vegetables mother never had.

1972 in Numbers

Census Statistics [1]:

- Population of the world   3.85 billion
- Population in the United States   213.27 million
- Population in the United Kingdom   55.89 million
- Population in Canada   22.07 million
- Population in Australia   13.24 million
- Average age for marriage of women   20.9 years old
- Average age for marriage of men   23.3 years old
- Average family income USA $11,120 per year
- Unemployment rate USA   5.2 %

Costs of Goods [2]:

- Average new house — $27,299
- Average new car — $3,760
- Cadillac Fleetwood Eldorado — $7,180
- A gallon of gasoline — $0.36
- A loaf of bread — $0.33
- Butter — $0.75 per pound
- Sugar — $0.10 per pound
- Oranges, Florida — $0.55 for 10
- Sliced ham — $0.39 per pound
- Mayonnaise, Kraft — $0.64 quart jar
- Potatoes — $0.12 per pound
- Fresh eggs — $0.39 per dozen
- Soap, Ivory — $0.23 for 4 bars
- A cinema ticket — $1.50

---

1 Figures taken from worldometers.info/world-population, US National Center for Health Statistics, Divorce and Divorce Rates US (cdc.gov/nchs/data/series/sr_21/sr21_029.pdf) and United States Census Bureau, Historical Marital Status Tables (census.gov/data/tables/time-series/demo/families/marital.html).
2 Figures from thepeoplehistory.com, mclib.info/reference/local-history & dqydj.com/historical-home-prices/.

Advertisement

The great getaway machines.
Leave behind the regimented week that was, to be continued another day.
Til then, get away and sort things out and be with friends on your Yamaha Enduros.
125cc and 175cc Enduros.
Light, quick, easy to handle, yet, like all Yamaha dual-purpose machines, they're built tough to take you off the road and over the trails leading back to quiet meadows and peaceful skies.
Yamaha Enduros.
The weekend getaway machines that have earned the right to be called "Great."
See them at your Yamaha dealer. Before next Saturday.
YAMAHA The great machines for '72.

Switch from what you're used to.

Would you like to become less dependent on cigarettes? Would you like to smoke less? Or inhale less?

Then you ought to think about switching to new Dutch Treats. The filtered little cigar with a taste that's different from cigarettes but very satisfying.

Dutch Treats could change the way you smoke.

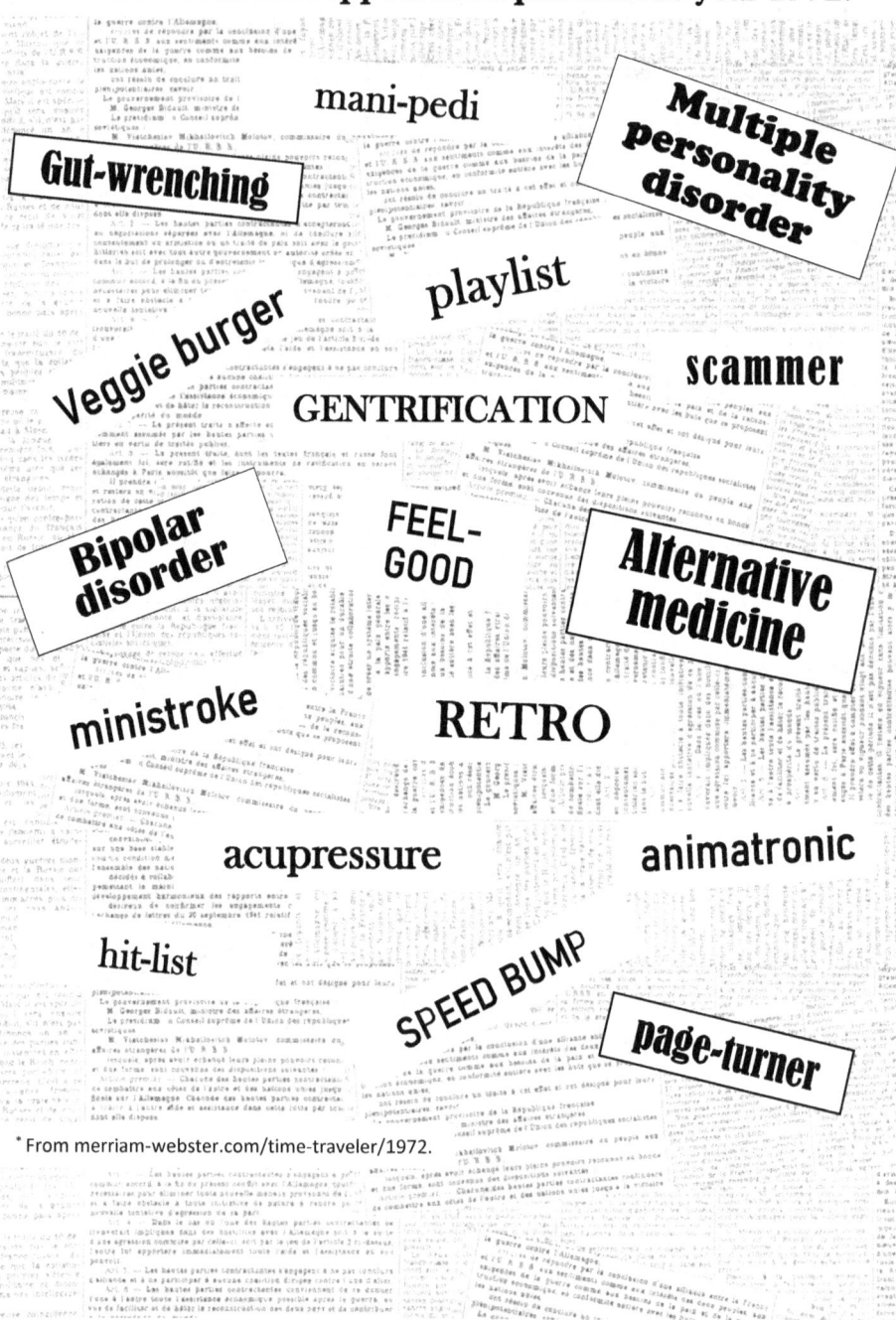

A heartfelt plea from the author:

I sincerely hope you enjoyed reading this book and that it brought back many fond memories from the past.

Success as an author has become increasingly difficult with the proliferation of **AI generated** copycat books by unscrupulous sellers. They are clever enough to escape copyright action and use dark web tactics to secure paid-for **fake reviews**, something I would never do.

Hence I would like to ask you — I plead with you — the reader, to leave a star rating or review on Amazon. This helps make my book discoverable for new readers, and helps me to compete fairly against the devious copycats.

If this book was a gift to you, you can leave stars or a review on your own Amazon account, or you can ask the gift-giver or a family member to do this on your behalf.

I have enjoyed researching and writing this book for you and would greatly appreciate your feedback.

Best regards,
Bernard Bradforsand-Tyler.

Please leave a
book review/rating at:

https://bit.ly/1972-reviews

Or scan the QR code:

Flashback books make the perfect gift- see the full range at

https://bit.ly/FlashbackSeries

Image Attributions

Photographs and images used in this book are reproduced courtesy of the following:

Page 6 – From *Life* Mag 10th Mar 1972. Source: books.google.com/books?id=d1IEAAAAMBAJ&printsec. (PD image).*
Page 8 – Young family, image by u/19blackdog72. Source: reddit.com/r/OldSchoolCool/.
Page 9 – Canal Soda Pop Festival, Labour Day, 1972. From the Sonny Brown collection, MSS 228-0005. – Peace March to Kezar Stadium, 22nd April 1972, creator unknown. Source: foundsf.org/index.php?title=Peace_March_to_Kezar_1972. From OpenSFHistory.org wnp28.3239. – Sorority sisters, creator and date unknown. Source: reddit.com/r/OldSchoolCool/. Pre-1978, no renewed copyright. (PD image).
Page 10 – From *Life* Mag 3rd Nov 1972. Source: books.google.com/books?id=uVYEAAAAMBAJ&printsec. (PD image).*
Page 11 – Photos circa 1971, creators unknown. Sources: reddit.com/r/OldSchoolCool/comments/890bq6/ and daemen.edu/about/fast-facts/college-history-timeline. Pre 1978, no renewed copyright. (PD image).
Page 12 – Photos unknown creators. Sources: flashbak.com/glorious-colour-photographs-of-london-in-1972-379690/ and chroniclelive.co.uk/lifestyle/nostalgia/gallery/7033628. Pre-1978, no copyright mark (PD image).
Page 13 – Women's Liberation protest 8th Nov 1971. Source: redflagwalks.wordpress.com/category/womens-liberation/. – Boy crossing road, date and creator unknown. Both images this page pre-1978, no mark (PD image).
Page 14 – From *Life* Mag 10th Nov 1972. Source: books.google.com/books?id=8VQEAAAAMBAJ&printsec (PD image).*
Page 15– Gay Pride march, by LSE Library. Source: commons.wikimedia.org/wiki/Category:Pride_London_1972. Pre-1978, no copyright mark (PD image). – Engineers strike, 1973, creator unknown. Pre-1978, no mark (PD image).
Page 16 – Commune members, source: allthatsinteresting.com/hippie-communes.
– Commune members pose in front of a tipi, by John Olson from Life Magazine, 18th Jul 1969. Source: books.google.com/books?id=K08EAAAAMBAJ&printsec.
Page 17 – Tending to the fields, source: burlingtonfreepress.com/story/news/local/vermont/2015/07/24/vermont-remains-hippie-epicenter/30564907/, photo by Rebecca Lepkoff of Vermont Historical Society. – Geodesic dome, source: vpr.org/post/communes-hippie-invasion-and-how-1970s-changed-state#stream/0 by Kate Daloz. – Commune bus, source: allthatsinteresting.com/hippie-communes. All images this page pre-1978, no copyright mark (PD image).
Page 18 – From *Hot Rod Magazine* April 1972. Source: flickr.com/photos/91591049@N00/13241397855/ by SenseiAlan. Attribution 4.0 International. (CC BY 4.0).
Page 19 – Friday afternoon traffic heading out of Atlanta, by Al Stephenson / AJC file. Source: ajc.com/lifestyles/flashback-photos-through-the-years-1951-1997/ByK7dbup2R66nM4TMIWX9O/. – Southpark Mall aerial photo, creator unknown. Pre-1978, no copyright mark (PD image).
Page 20 – 1972 Yenko Vega Stinger GT, source: flickr.com/photos/autohistorian/35720512371/ by Alden Jewel. Attribution 4.0 International (CC BY 4.0). – 1972 Buick Century, source unknown. Pre-1978, no mark (PD image).
– Chevrolet Vega from *Car Craft Magazine* June 1972. Source: flickr.com/photos/91591049@N00/13058212935/ by SenseiAlan. Attribution 4.0 International (CC BY 4.0).
Page 21 – Mark II Toyota from *Life* Magazine 1st Sep 1972. Source: books.google.com/books?id=H1cEAAAAMBAJ&printsec. (PD image).* – 1972 Datsun 1200 Sport Coupe. Source: flickr.com/photos/autohistorian/32260363001/ by Alden Jewell. Attribution 4.0 International (CC BY 4.0). – 1972 BMW Beetle from *Life* Magazine 28th Jan 1972. Source: books.google.com/books?id=D0AEAAAAMBAJ&printsec. (PD image).*
Page 22 – Source: flickr.com/photos/52131045@N03/21739663214/ by Vance. Attribution 4.0 Internat. (CC BY 4.0).
Page 23 – Ford Mustang1972 ad. Source: classiccarstodayonline.com/classic-car-print-advertisements/. (PD image).*
Page 24 – Source: latimes.com/local/california/la-me-lopez-la-better-worse-20180825-story. Pre-1978. – Chart: epa.gov/ transportation-air-pollution-and-climate-change/accomplishments-and-success-air-pollution-transportation.
Page 25 – Sources: insider.com/vintage-photos-los-angeles-smog-pollution-epa-2020-1. – commons.wikimedia.org/wiki/File:Two_California_Plaza_-_350_S._Grand_Avenue,_Los_Angeles. – commons.wikimedia.org/wiki/File:EAST_RIVER_AND_MANHATTAN_SKYLINE_IN_HEAVY_SMOG_-_NARA_-_548365. – quora.com/What-does-the-British-phrase-it-was-a-real-pea-souper-mean. All images this page are pre-1978, no copyright mark (PD image).
Page 26 – From *Life* Mag 8th Sep 1972. Source: books.google.com/books?id=WIUEAAAAMBAJ&printsec (PD image).*
Page 27 – *Operation Crossroads*, Bikini Atoll, 25th July 1946. Source: en.wikipedia.org/wiki/Operation_Crossroads.
– *Small Boy* at Nevada Proving Grounds, 14th July 1962. Source: commons.wikimedia.org/wiki/File:Small_Boy_nuclear_test_1962.jpg. All photos this page by either US Army or Navy and are in the public domain. (PD images).
Page 28 – Battle of An Loc, April 1972. Photo is the work of a US Federal employee. Source: commons.wikimedia.org/wiki/Category:Easter_Offensive (PD image). – Children at play in Kontum, South Vietnam, Dec 1972, by Lấy từ ảnh của A. Abbas. Source: Abbas Attar/ Magnum Photos. Pre-1978, no copyright mark (PD image).
Page 29 – San Francisco peace march, 22nd April 1972. Photos by OpenSFHistory.org wnp28.3268 and wnp28.3240. source: foundsf.org/index.php?title=Peace_March_to_Kezar_1972. – Fonda press conference 18th Jan 1975. Source: commons. wikimedia.org/wiki/File:Jane_Fonda_1975c by Mieremet, Rob / Anefo. From the Dutch National Archives. All (PD images).
Page 30 – Newspaper articles from the 1970s and movie posters by Warner Bros. and 20th Century Fox. (PD images).**
Page 31 – From *Life* Mag 10th Mar 1972. Source: books.google.com/books?id=d1IEAAAAMBAJ&printsec. (PD image).*

Page 32 – Republican arrests, creators unknown. Source: anphoblacht.com/contents/26282. Pre-1978, no copyright mark (PD images). – Peace Wall by Robin Kirk, 2008. Source: flickr.com/photos/rightsatduke/4595426547/. Attribution 4.0 International (CC BY 4.0).
Page 33 – Bloody Sunday riots, creator unknown. Source: allocine.fr/article/dossiers/cinema/dossier-18591398/and thetimes.co.uk/article/bloody-sunday-paratrooper-fired-as-if-on-turkey-shoot-2klcfqhqz. Pre-1978, no mark (PD images).
Page 35 – From Life Mag 6th Oct 1972. Source: books.google.com/books?id=aVUEAAAAMBAJ&printsec (PD image).*
Page 36 – From Life Mag 28th Jan 1972. Source: books.google.com/books?id=D0AEAAAAMBAJ&printsec (PD image).*
Page 37– Gough Whitlam, property of Australian Information Services, courtesy of the National Library of Australia, PIC Box PIC/8128 #PIC/8128/nla.obj-147274193. – Whitlam in China, creator and date unknown. All pre-1978 (PD images).
Page 38 – Opening Ceremony, Munich, Germany, 16th July 1972. Creator unknown. Source: olympics.com/en/olympic-games/munich-1972. – Günter Zahn lights the cauldron. Source: zdf.de/nachrichten/sport/olympia-tokio-muenchen-1972-fackel-guenter-zahn-102.html. All images this page pre-1978, no copyright mark (PD images).
Page 39 – Images during and after the hostage crisis at the Munich Olympics, 1972. All images this page are the property of Associated Press and are used here under fair use terms as they are important to the article written and free images are not available. These are low-resolution images. It is believed that these images will not devalue the ability of the copyright holder to profit from the original work and are too small to be used to make illegal copies for use in another book.
Page 40 – Golda Meir by IDF Spokesperson's Unit. Source: commons.wikimedia.org/wiki/Category:Golda_Meir_in_1973. Attribution-ShareAlike 3.0 Unported (CC BY-SA 3.0). – Poster for Munich by Universal Pictures.**
Page 41 – American Airlines 707 print advertisement, source: eBay.com. (PD image).*
Page 42 – Zenith Space Command collection print advertisement, source: eBay.com. (PD image).*
Page 43 – Promotional photo for Grease, original cast 1972. – Film poster by Paramount Pictures,** 1978.
Page 44 – All in the Family screen still, 4th May 1971, by CBS Television.**
Source: en.wikipedia.org/wiki/All_in_the_Family #/media/File: Archie_and_Lionel_All_in_the_Family_1971.JPG.
Page 45 – Still image and poster from the TV series Hawaii Five-0 by CBS, 1970.** – Marcus Welby MD. cast, source: commons.wikimedia.org/wiki/File: Marcus_Welby_MD_cast.JPG. Pre-1978, no copyright mark (PD image).
Page 46 – M*A*S*H main cast photo by CBS. 1st Sep 1972. Source: commons.wikimedia.org/wiki/Category:M*A*S*H_(TV_series). – The Bob Newhart Show main cast photo by CBS. 31st May 1977. Source: commons.wikimedia.org/wiki/Category:The_Bob_Newhart_Show. – The Waltons publicity photo by CBS, 30th Sep 1976. Source: commons.wikimedia. org/wiki/File:The_Waltons_1976.JPG. – The Rookies main cast photo by Spelling-Goldberg Productions. 1st Aug 1973. Source: commons.wikimedia.org/ wiki/Category:The_Rookies?uselang=it. All images this page Pre-1978, no copyright mark (PD image).
Page 47 – From Life Magazine 28th Jan 1972: books.google.com/books?id=D0AEAAAAMBAJ&printsec (PD image).*
Page 48 – Still images from Mean Streets by Warner Bros,** 1973. and The Godfather by Paramount Pictures,** 1972.
Page 49 & 50 – Film posters for the movies The Godfather by Paramount Pictures, 1972.** Cabaret by Allied Artists Pictures, 1972.** What's Up Doc? by Warner Brothers, 1972.** – The Poseidon Adventure by 20th Century Fox, 1972.** – The Towering Inferno by 20th Century Fox and Warner Bros, 1974.** – Earthquake by Universal Pictures, 1974.** – Tidal Wave by Toho Company, 1973.**
Page 51 – From Life Magazine 6th Oct 1972: books.google.com/books?id=aVUEAAAAMBAJ&printsec (PD image).*
Page 52 – Elton in Hamburg, Germany, Mar 1972. Source: commons.wikimedia.org/wiki/Category:Elton_John_in_1972. Permission CC BY-SA 2.0. – Stevie Wonder by MoTown Records, 21st Aug 1973. Source: commons.wikimedia.org/wiki/Category:Stevie_ onder_in_1973. Pre-1978, no copyright mark (PD image). – Marvin Gaye by MoTown Records. Date unknown. Pre-1978, no copyright mark (PD image).
Page 53 – Jagger & Richards Winterland in San Francisco (California, USA) June 1972. Source: commons.wikimedia. org/wiki/Category:The_Rolling_Stones_in_1972. Permission CC BY-SA 2.0. – Helen Reddy, publicity photo from The Carol Burnett Show, Oct 1973. Source: commons.wikimedia.org/wiki/Category:Helen_Reddy_in_1973. – David Bowie as Ziggy Stardust, by Brian Duffy from the Duffy Archive & The David Bowie Archive. This is a small reproductin low-resolution image for information only, reproduced under fair use terms. The image is relevant to the article, and it is believed this image will not devalue the ability of the copyright holders to profit from the original works.
Page 54 – Roberta Flack by Atlantic Records, 1976. Source: commons.wikimedia.org/wiki/Category:Roberta_Flack. – Sammy Davis Jr., date and creator unknown. – Don McLean publicity photo for Herbert S. Gart management, 20th Feb 1976. Source: commons.wikimedia.org/wiki/Category:Don_McLean. – Withers in a 1971 ad for Just as I Am by Sussex Records. Source: Billboard, 9th Oct 1971. All photos this page are pre-1978, no copyright marks (PD images).
Page 55 – Neil Young promotional photo by Warner/Reprise. Source: commons.wikimedia.org/wiki/Category:Neil_Young. – Neil Diamond performing at Woburn Abbey in Bedfordshire, England 2nd July 1977. Photo by Skybird73. Source: commons.wikimedia.org/wiki/Category:Neil_Diamond. Photos this page are pre-1978, no marks (PD images).

Page 56 – The Sony All-Weather Radio print advertisement, source: eBay.com. (PD image).*
Page 57 – From *Life* Mag 21st Apr 1972. Source: books.google.com/books?id=LUAEAAAAMBAJ&printsec (PD image).*
Page 58 – Pants and skirt-suit, 1969, creator unknown. Pre-1978, (PD image).– Maxi-dress by YSL, Spring-Summer 1969. Source: minniemuse.com/articles/creative-connections/ patchwork. Pre-1978, (PD image).
Page 59 – Elizabeth Taylor, source: instyle.com/celebrity/transformations/elizabeth-taylors-changing-looks. – Thea Porter dress, photographer Patrick Hunt, 1970. – Weipert and Burda fashion show, Apr 1972, photo by Friedrich Magnussen. Permission CC BY-SA 3.0 DE. – Mini dresses, sources: pinterest.com/pin/99782947967669796/ and retrospace.org/2011_01_01_archive.html unknown photographers. Pre-1978, no copyright mark (PD image).
Page 60 – Fashions from Sears Catalogues, Pre-1978, no copyright mark (PD image). – Hungarian singer Szűcs Judit wears embroidered demin. Source: commons.wikimedia.org/wiki/File:Szűcs_Judit_énekesnő._Fortepan_88657.jpg. Licensed under the Creative Commons Attribution-Share Alike 3.0 Unported. – Knit polyester pants from the 1975 J.C. Penney catalog. Pre-1978, no copyright marks (PD image). – Flared jumpsuits, creator unknown. Pre-1978, no marks (PD image).
Page 61 – From *Life* Mag 12th May 1972. Source: books.google.com/books?id=U1UEAAAAMBAJ&printsec (PD image).*
Page 62 – Sears Jeans Advertisement from *Playboy* Sep 1972. Source: flickr.com/photos/91591049@N00/25413932706/ by SenseiAlan. Attribution 4.0 International (CC BY 4.0).
Page 63 – Nik Nik shirts, polyester jumpsuits, and knit pantsuits, source: onedio.com/haber/erkekte-retro-modasinin-tutmamasinin-32-mantikli-sebebi-300983. – Polyester tops and pants, toweling jumpsuits, and shrink tops by Colombia Minerva, source: flashbak.com/the-good-the-bad-and-the-tacky-20-fashion-trends-of-the-1970s-26213/. – Denim on denim source: typesofjeanfits.com/a-brief-history-of-jeans-denim-history-timeline/. – Safari suits source: klyker.com/ 1970s-fashion/. All images this page Pre-1978, no copyright mark or renewal (PD image).
Page 64 – Still image from the film *Saturday Night Fever* by Paramount Pictures.** Source: vocal.media/beat/the-list-saturday-night-fever-40th-anniversary. – Dancers Studio 54, sources: definition.org/studio-54/2/ & alexilubomirski.com/image-collections/studio-54. Pre-1978, no copyright marks (PD image).
Page 65 – Canada Dry advertisement, source: etsy.com. (PD image).*
Page 66 – From *Life* Magazine 3rd Nov 1972: books.google.com/books?id=uVYEAAAAMBAJ&printsec (PD image).*
Page 67 – Jack Nicklaus, creator unknown. Source: prosportsmemorabilia.com. Pre-1978 (PD image). – Boston Marathon, 1972, from Bettman Corbis. This is a low-resolution image for information only, reproduced under fair use terms. It is believed this image will not devalue the ability of the copyright holders to profit from the original works. – King in 2016, by Jonathan Exley. Source: commons.wikimedia.org/wiki/Category:Billie_Jean_King. Pre-1978 (PD image).
Page 68 – From Life Mag 2nd Jun 1972. Source: books.google.com/books?id=ClcEAAAAMBAJ&printsec. (PD image).*
Page 69 – Artist impression *Pioneer 10* by NASA, Source: nasa.gov/directorates/heo/scan/images/history/March1972. html (PD image). – Hamilton *Pulsar*, creator unknown. – Polaroid SX-70 source: en.wikipedia.org/wiki/Polaroid_SX-70#/media/ File:Polaroid_SX-70_(4462345243).jpg. CC0 1.0 Universal (PD image).
Page 70 & 71 – Shōichi Yokoi in 1945 and 1972. Source:commons.wikimedia.org/wiki/Category:Sh%C5%8Dichi_Yokoi. – Nixon and Zhou Enlai. Source: en.wikipedia.org/wiki/1972_visit_by_Richard_Nixon_to_China. – Idi Amin at the UN, 1975. Source: commons.wikimedia.org/wiki/Category:Idi_Amin. – President Marcos, 17th Oct 2008. Source: commons.wikimedia. org/wiki/Category:Ferdinand_Marcos. – Joseph Biden official Presidential portrait, 2nd March 2021. Source: commons.wikimedia.org/wiki/Joe_Biden. All images these pages pre-1978, no copyright mark (PD images).
Page 72-74 – All photos are, where possible, CC BY 2.0 or PD images made available by the creator for free use including commercial use. Where commercial use photos are unavailable, photos are included here for information only under US fair use laws due to: 1- images are low resolution copies; 2- images do not devalue the ability of the copyright holders to profit from the original works in any way; 3- Images are too small to be used to make illegal copies for use in another book; 4- The images are relevant to the article created.
Page 75 – From Life Mag 1st Sep 1972. Source: books.google.com/books?id=H1cEAAAAMBAJ&printsec. (PD image).*
Page 78 – From *Playboy* Magazine Sep 1972. Source: flickr.com/photos/91591049@N00/25226833954/in/photostream/ by SenseiAlan. Attribution 4.0 International (CC BY 4.0).
Page 79 – Dutch Treats Little Cigars print advertisement, source: eBay.com. (PD image).*

*Advertisement (or image from an advertisement) is in the public domain because it was published in a collective work (such as a periodical issue) in the US between 1925 and 1977 and without a copyright notice specific to the advertisement.
**Posters for movies or events are either in the public domain (published in the US between 1925 and 1977 and without a copyright notice specific to the artwork) or owned by the production company, creator, or distributor of the movie or event. Posters, where not in the public domain, and screen stills from movies or TV shows, are reproduced here under USA Fair Use laws due to: 1- images are low resolution copies; 2- images do not devalue the ability of the copyright holders to profit from the original works in any way; 3- Images are too small to be used to make illegal copies for use in another book; 4- The images are relevant to the article created.

This book was written by Bernard Bradforsand-Tyler as part of *A Time Traveler's Guide* series of books.

All rights reserved. The author exerts the moral right to be identified as the author of the work.

No parts of this book may be reproduced, stored in any retrieval system, or transmitted in any form or by any means, without prior written permission from the author.

This is a work of nonfiction. No names have been changed, no events have been fabricated. The content of this book is provided as a source of information for the reader, however it is not meant as a substitute for direct expert opinion. Although the author has made every effort to ensure that the information in this book is correct at time of printing, and while this publication is designed to provide accurate information in regard to the subject matters covered, the author assumes no responsibility for errors, inaccuracies, omissions, or any other inconsistencies herein and hereby disclaims any liability to any party for any loss, damage, or disruption caused by errors or omissions.

All images contained herein are reproduced with the following permissions:
- Images included in the public domain.
- Images obtained under creative commons license.
- Images included under fair use terms.
- Images reproduced with owner's permission.

All image attributions and source credits are provided at the back of the book. All images are the property of their respective owners and are protected under international copyright laws.

First printed in 2021 in the USA (ISBN 978-1-922676-00-9).
Revised in 2024, 2nd Edition (978-1-922676-25-2).
Self-published by B. Bradforsand-Tyler.

www.ingramcontent.com/pod-product-compliance
Lightning Source LLC
Chambersburg PA
CBHW050208130526
44590CB00043B/3318